A. W. Tozer was one of the great spiritual giants of the past century and he comes to life again in the pages of this masterful biography by Lyle Dorsett. Here we see how the jewels from Tozer's pen were ᵣₑ____ _____ f his life. This is a book that will bring ever

TIMOTHY GEORGE
Founding Dean of Beeson Divinity Schoo
Senior Editor of *Christianity Today*

Lyle Dorsett has done it again. I found myself absorbed with this realistic biography of A.W. Tozer, a man whose writings have blessed us all of us. In these pages we are invited to walk with a man who passionately pursued God but at the same time had obvious faults, particularly in his relationship with his family. Tozer's life also introduces us to the various battles that the church was fighting in the forties and fifties, and how evangelicals responded to them. This book encourages us by reminding us that God uses imperfect but God-focused people to bless His church and strengthen the saints. Read this book and you'll find yourself recommending it to your friends.

DR. ERWIN LUTZER
Pastor, Moody Church, Chicago

Lyle Dorsett has performed a great service in producing this fascinating new biography of A. W. Tozer, a simple, self-educated midwesterner who began his working life in an Akron, Ohio, rubber factory. It tells the remarkable story of how this young man came in contact with the literature of Christian devotion, absorbed it deeply, and then, with a uniquely engaging style (half Jeremiah, half Mark Twain), passed along his discovered insights to countless soul-hungry Americans. Two of his many works, *The Pursuit of God* and *The Knowledge of the Holy*, remain classics today. *A Passion for God* will be an essential companion to all who wish to tap into a remarkable spiritual legacy.

GLEN G. SCORGIE, PhD
Professor of Theology, Bethel Seminary San Diego
Author of *A Little Guide to Christian Spirituality* (2007)

Lyle Dorsett's biography of my grandfather, A.W. Tozer, is the complete source for anyone who would like to learn about and understand the person, heart, and passion of Dr. Tozer. For my first ten years of life I was able to know him as a grandfather. As time went by I began to learn of and understand his public life and his place among Christians. The more I knew the more I realized I had only pieces of the story. Dr. Dorsett has provided that and more in this wonderfully detailed look into Dr. Tozer's life and ministry.

PAUL TOZER
Grandson of A. W. Tozer

From Moses to Peter and Luther to Spurgeon, even the most gifted and accomplished servants of the Lord have had their blemishes (don't we all?) and we can learn from them. This book introduces us to some of the more private aspects of Dr. Tozer's life and ministry, and while it may disturb some, it should also encourage all of us to examine our own lives and aim for God's best.

WARREN W. WIERSBE, Author
Former pastor of Moody Church, Chicago

As with so many, A. W. Tozer's writings were a fiery landmark in my spiritual growth and my love for God. Lyle Dorsett's magnificent *A Passion for God* recalls and rekindles those fires. This is a fascinating and pleasurable and profitable read!

R. KENT HUGHES
Senior Pastor Emeritus
College Church in Wheaton

Lyle Dorsett captures the heart of the man whose life was totally focused on his pursuit of God. The opinions and feelings of his contemporaries, of those in his churches, or of even his own family, all took second place to his overwhelming passion to know Christ. Through this carefully researched and objectively written book, we have an intimate and unbiased look into the life of a man whose writings have resonated with God seekers around the world. A sidelight of the book is an inside look at the history of the Christian and Missionary Alliance through a man who catapulted the name of the Alliance around the world through his writings. In Dorsett's writings we see Tozer, first and foremost a man of prayer, a man oblivious to this world, a man with an earnest desire to seek and know God above all else.

JANET KUHNS HOWARD
Missionary with Christian and Missionary Alliance in Indonesia and member of the Christian and Missionary Alliance Board of Directors

For those who hunger to know the Lord in a deeper way, Lyle Dorsett's masterful account of A. W. Tozer's spiritual journey will encourage, inspire and challenge. This book is simply a must read for serious Christians.

JOHN WOODBRIDGE
Research Professor of Church History
Trinity Evangelical Divinity School

LYLE DORSETT

A Passion for God

THE SPIRITUAL JOURNEY OF

A. W. TOZER

MOODY PUBLISHERS

CHICAGO

©2008

LYLE DORSETT

Editor: Pam Pugh
Interior Design: Ragont Design
Cover Design: Paetzold Associates Inc.
Cover Photo: Courtesy of Lowell Tozer

Library of Congress Cataloging-in-Publication Data

Dorsett, Lyle W.
     A passion for God : the spiritual journey of A. W. Tozer / Lyle Dorsett.
       p. cm.
     Includes bibliographical references.
     ISBN-13: 978-0-8024-8133-7
     ISBN-10: 0-8024-8133-7
     1. Tozer, A. W. (Aiden Wilson), 1897–1963. 2. Christian and
Missionary Alliance—2. United States—Clergy—Biography. I. Title.

BX6700.Z8D67 2008
289.9—dc22
[B]
                                                                2007044364

We hope you enjoy this book from Moody Publishers. Our goal is to provide high-quality, thought-provoking books and products that connect truth to your real needs and challenges. For more information on other books and products written and produced from a biblical perspective, go to www.moodypublishers.com or write to:

Moody Publishers
820 N. LaSalle Boulevard
Chicago, IL 60610

1 3 5 7 9 10 8 6 4 2

Printed in the United States of America

*To my wife, best friend, and comrade in ministry, Mary; and
to our beloved son and daughter-in-law, Michael and Connie; and
our esteemed grandchildren whose love and laughter enrich our lives
Bill, Daniel, Elizabeth, and Henry*

CONTENTS

Acknowledgments

It is with genuine gratitude that I acknowledge a long list of people who have helped me write this book. First of all, I thank my wife and best friend, Mary, for immeasurable assistance. She helped with the research, offered hospitality to friends of Tozer whom I wished to interview, typed three drafts of the manuscript, offered much constructive criticism, and extended invaluable encouragement.

Next to Mary Dorsett, no one provided as much help as the late Harry Verploegh. We first met in 1996. He encouraged me to write a biography of A. W. Tozer, and he prodded me to interview dozens of Tozer's relatives and friends as quickly as possible. Although Mr. Verploegh knew I had several previous commitments and therefore could not actually write the book for some time, he counseled me to "interview the family and friends now. Like me," he insisted, "they all are getting older and it won't be long before the Lord rings the bell for us." Thanks to his insistence and the personal relationships he had with Tozer's family, colleagues, and acquaintances, over forty people were interviewed—several of whom received the call to heaven before this project was done.

Harry Verploegh's contributions, however, were even greater than his proddings and connections. He had been one of A. W. Tozer's closest friends for over thirty years and his own memories were extensive and rich. Furthermore, he gave me all of his files of Tozer-related documents, and he gathered correspondence and materials related to Tozer from several men—including extensive files from R. W. Battles who at one time had hoped to write Tozer's life story.

Thanks to Mr. Verploegh, I made contact with all seven of the Tozer children. Each one—Lowell, Forrest, Aiden Wendell Jr., Wendell, Rolland (Raleigh), Stanley, and Rebecca—granted me extensive and candid interviews. Wendell's wife, Connie, likewise shared some of her memories.

The following people—all friends, colleagues, or acquaintances of Mr. Tozer—generously answered questions and provided keen insights: Jim Adair, Anita Bailey, Robert Battles, R. S. Brown, Amelia Bryant, Gertrude Carlson, Isabelle Chase, David Enlow, Lloyd Erickson, K. Neill Foster, Paul Fromer, James Hay, Janet Kuhns Howard, Bernard King, Louis King and Mrs. Louis King, William Lemke, Mrs. Sir Louis, Ed Maxey, Clara Moore, Victor Oliver, Bill Palmer, Ruth Ranshaw, John Sawin, David Schmidt Sr., Gerald Smith, Harry Verploegh, and Ethel Wolfe.

I could never have conducted such an extensive oral history project in a relatively short time without the able help of two research assistants. First, Donald Shepson, a personal friend who was serving as an associate pastor in a Christian and Missionary Alliance Church in Florida, conducted many interviews with people who lived near him at Shell Point Village, a senior retirement village. Second, my friend and former graduate student Robert Henry transcribed and conducted several interviews and located many primary sources.

A research grant from Wheaton College enabled me to employ students to gather data. I am indebted to David Dykes, Jake Hanson, and Kristin Kano for their help.

During his last year in the Master of Divinity program at Beeson Divinity School, Samford University, Marshall Wilmhoff—who loves the writings of A. W. Tozer as much as I—volunteered countless hours to help me sort and photocopy every article that Tozer wrote for *The Alliance Weekly*. Mr. Wilmhoff not only saved me innumerable hours of work, he became a good friend who talked with me about Tozer's ministry and offered a helpful critique of an early draft of the book manuscript.

A generous group of people answered my author's query in *Alliance Life*. The following people sent me their files of old issues of *The Alliance Weekly*, autographs, photographs, and personal correspondence and reminiscences of Tozer: Martha Dougherty, Charles Eumurian, Marilyn Frederickson, Velma Hatoski, Jane Kenney, Ester Lott, Francis Wilson, and Homer Yiengst.

Phil Shappard, broadcast technology manager at Moody Broadcasting Network shared his vast knowledge of Tozer's recorded sermons, and he provided copies of many recordings.

No author can work with a better team than the talented, efficient, and delightful people at Moody Publishers. First of all, I am indebted to Greg Thornton, vice president of Publications, for his confidence in me and this project. I am also grateful for the superb critical and editorial work of Lisa Major and Pam Pugh.

Paul Erickson and Bob Shuster at the Billy Graham Center Archives and David Malone of Wheaton College Archives offered valuable aid to me and my research assistants, as did the staffs at the Presbyterian Historical Society, and the public library personnel in Indianapolis, Indiana; Toledo, Ohio; Clearfield County, Pennsylvania; and Ross County, Ohio. The people at the Christian and Missionary Alliance Archives at Colorado Springs were also very helpful.

I thank Catherine Sorich who owns one of the houses where the Tozers lived in Chicago. She allowed me to take pictures and study both house and property.

Any errors of facts or interpretations are mine, but I owe a large debt to Professor Lowell Tozer and his wife, Alison Lawrance, for their careful and critical reading of the manuscript. I am also grateful to Aidan W. Tozer Jr. and Carol Tozer Delfino for their very helpful comments.

Finally, I thank Dr. Timothy George and Dr. Paul House, my dean and associate dean respectively, at Beeson Divinity School, Samford University, for providing research funds that enabled me to make two trips and acquire some materials that afforded me the opportunity to put the finishing touches on this book.

Foreword

One of the most influential and least recognized evangelical spokesmen of the twentieth century was A. W. Tozer. No headliner in the popular media, no megachurch celebrity; his significance was in the spiritual depth of his biblical message.

Like the prophets of old, he proclaimed the Word of God as he understood it without compromise. His call was clear—repent from all sin, wholeheartedly embrace the cross, and follow Jesus in complete obedience. He believed that by divine grace, through faith in the precious blood and by the sanctifying power of the Holy Spirit, we could live victoriously in Christ every day. To be sure, this chosen way would not be easy, but never boring. For running through it all was the joy of personal communion with God and the experience of true worship.

Though he was sometimes criticized as being too mystical, too radical, people could see in his simple lifestyle, unencumbered by a quest for fame or fortune, a sincere desire to live by his convictions. However, virtually unknown were the struggles and loneliness out of which his preaching flowed. Many heard his sermons, many more read his books, yet few knew the inner man. Even those persons who were closest to him longed to know him better.

That is why I am grateful for this book. Dr. Lyle Dorsett, distinguished historian and beloved teacher, has given us a penetrating insight into Tozer's life and work. We see a very human person, his strengths as well as his weaknesses, and with keen sensitivity, the author brings out the qualities that went into the making of this unassuming saint.

Moreover, in telling the story, he opens a window into the storehouse of the riches of grace, showing what God can do in the heart of a man surrendered to Him. And by that same mighty power, what God did for Tozer He will do for any person who will lay aside self-centered indulgence of the flesh and seek to live for the glory of God.

Sobering reading. More than informational, I recommend it as good medicine for the soul.

Robert E. Coleman
Distinguished Professor
of Evangelism and Discipleship
Gordon-Conwell Theological Seminary

1

"I've Had a Lonely Life"

On Friday, May 17, 1963, hundreds of mourners attended a memorial service in Chicago to pay their respects to A. W. Tozer, the sixty-six-year-old pastor, teacher, and writer who had unexpectedly died at 12:45 a.m. the previous Sunday in a Toronto hospital. Although Aiden Tozer had lived and ministered from a Christian and Missionary Alliance Church in Toronto for four years, Christians in metropolitan Chicago still claimed him as their own. Consequently, despite the fact that there had already been a service in Toronto two days earlier, the Tozer family acquiesced to the desires of many Windy City people to publicly grieve and pay respect to the preacher who had ministered to them for thirty-five years.

Memorial service eulogies, letters of condolence, statements from Christian organizations, and hushed words among the bereaved, all expressed a similar sentiment of gratitude to Almighty God for sending a modern prophet. A. W. Tozer had called them to heartfelt confession, urged them to genuine repentance, pushed them to radical obedience, helped them to know God intimately, and led them up to the Heavenly Throne with praise.

Aiden W. Tozer directed people's attention toward God through almost every means of communication available in the early and middle twentieth century. He employed pulpits and platforms for forty-seven years, wrote hundreds of articles for periodicals over a span of four decades, conducted regular Saturday morning radio broadcasts over Chicago's WMBI for eight years, and published nine books during the last two decades of his life.

Dr. Tozer's messages pierced hearts and illumined minds with a profundity uncommon among Bible teachers and preachers. Indeed, spiritually alert people recognized that he possessed unique charisma—a sacred anointing. Those close to him explained that despite his busy schedule, the modern-day prophet spent several hours each day in prayer—not simply interceding but ardently seeking God's face and desiring to be in His presence. In brief, Dr. Tozer manifested the spiritual principle of 2 Chronicles 16:9: "The eyes of the Lord run to and fro throughout the whole earth, to show Himself strong on behalf of those whose heart is loyal to Him."

                   ⁖ ⁖ ⁖ ⁖ ⁖ ⁖ ⁖ ⁖ ⁖

It is nearly a half century ago that Aiden Wilson Tozer, one of the twentieth century's most enigmatic, complex, and profoundly anointed preachers, died in his sleep of a coronary thrombosis. He was all alone in a Toronto hospital, except for the Holy Spirit of Jesus Christ whom he knew and loved so passionately. This last scene of A. W. Tozer's life symbolized the way he lived during the forty-eight years following his conversion to faith in Jesus Christ.

From the time of his conversion in 1915 and his calling to preach in 1916, A. W. Tozer continually found himself surrounded by people. Nevertheless, this man who was raised in a large and extended family, married a godly woman who brought seven children into the world, and who lived most of his adult life preaching to large gatherings of people, confided to a friend in the 1950s: "I've had a lonely life."[1] Never one to use words carelessly, Tozer revealed this deep sadness during one of the few times he opened his most inmost being to anyone. But what an irony that Mr. Tozer lived a lonely life. He had a devoted wife and lovely children, all of whom would have treasured more personal intimacy. And among those throngs of listeners to his sermons, and many of the faithful members of the four churches he pastored, many would have stood in long lines for hours just to have a few minutes of personal time and intimate two-way sharing with the man who helped them know God but refused to let them know him.

A. W. Tozer died alone in a dark hospital room because he had urged Ada, his faithful wife of forty-five years, to go home and get some sleep. Indeed, he never wanted people to see him when he was ill and in bed. By choice he pushed people away in times of sickness as he often did in times of health. His family and closest friends all testified that Tozer, who magnetically attracted spiritually alert people who longed to know God, kept almost everyone he knew at a personal distance. Indeed, the only person who really *knew* Tozer, and with whom he spent long, quiet hours was the Holy Spirit—the only One with him during his final hours on earth.

If A. W. Tozer's loneliness was somewhat self-inflicted, there is another dimension of isolation that inevitably engulfs a man who faithfully preaches the whole counsel of Scripture. A. W. Tozer heralded biblical truth. He loved the Bible and unflinchingly preached what he believed people needed to hear, regardless of what they wanted. Furthermore, this self-educated preacher and teacher read deeply of the early church fathers, and he sought to interpret the Scriptures within the context of how they were interpreted and applied throughout church history. Consequently, Tozer was nonsectarian. He found riches in Christian tradition—riches sometimes overlooked by teachers and preachers who were confident that nothing written between the book of Acts and the Reformation, with the possible exception of St. Augustine, could be useful to true disciples of Jesus Christ.

Tozer's enthusiasm for the writings of the many so-called Christian mystics distressed still other faithful people. To the minds of many of Tozer's generation a mystic could not be Christian. They feared "mysticism" was a way to smuggle Eastern paganism into the church. But Tozer begged to differ. He frequently asked, "How can anyone have a 'personal relationship' with Jesus Christ today unless it is mystical?" Tozer insisted that Jesus does not walk our streets as He walked the roads of Galilee. "Eternal life is to *know* the Father and Jesus Christ whom He has sent" (see John 17:3), and only a mystical relationship can enable one to have this grace of intimacy and knowledge.[2] In brief, A. W. Tozer's teaching on the "deeper life"—that is a relationship with God that is only opened up and sustained through the person of the Holy Spirit—caused some people who otherwise admired him to be a bit wary of his teaching on the Holy Spirit.

Like the ancient Hebrew prophets, Tozer alienated religious leaders. He spoke publicly of his disdain for materialism, consumerism, and worldliness, wherever he detected it infiltrating the church. This led to no end of criticism.

Since Tozer's death this problem of worldliness in American culture and in the church has grown much more pronounced. Consequently, his writings are still anathema to people who share the Western mania of consumer Christianity. In fact, by twentieth- and early twenty-first-century standards of success, A. W. Tozer is scarcely worthy of notice. In a nation that celebrates rapid, sustained, and quantifiable growth as primary measuring sticks of value, Tozer's name will not be found on the rosters of role models or in the pantheon of heroes, even within the hallowed halls of many American seminaries or within the training programs of institutional churches.

A. W. Tozer's relative obscurity is the result of several factors. First of all, he spoke prophetically to the church, and historically we see that the religious leaders of any era seldom admire those sent to them with words of truth. Like prophets of old, the thin, mustached, and bespectacled herald of truth who originally came from the hilly wilderness of western Pennsylvania, spoke with razor-like sharpness. He admonished Christian leaders for their drift toward worldliness manifested in growing practices of adopting leadership models from the business world for the church and for allowing various forms of entertainment to take the place of biblical preaching, teaching, and theocentric worship. Many church leaders did not like his critique of their practices during his lifetime, and their worldly offspring today find his criticisms even less palatable, especially since so many have enthusiastically and unquestionably adopted the precise methods he found so deplorable. Second, the cult of success is so firmly entrenched in the contemporary institutional church that many leaders see Tozer as simply irrelevant. With our turn-of-the-century obsession to attract crowds and make them comfortable for fear they will leave, Tozer's prophetic calls for radical obedience to Christ, personal holiness, purposive and passionate prayer life, spartan lifestyles, and God-centered worship, caused him to sound—in the minds of many people—insensitive, unloving, and in some cases downright abrasive. Finally, due to the market-driven contemporary church's love affair with growth, fostered by "seeker friendly" services, "inoffensivism" in the pulpit, church growth courses in the seminaries, and continuing education conferences for pastors on how to build bigger churches, few are inclined to examine the life and ministry of a man who served as a pastor for forty-four years but never attracted and sustained a congregation of more than four or five hundred people.[3]

A. W. Tozer was neither hurt nor surprised by his relative obscurity in comparison to some of his highly acclaimed contemporaries who commanded large annual salaries and substantial honorariums for outside speaking engagements. On the contrary, Tozer poked fun at himself and laughingly remarked that he preached himself off of nearly every camp meeting and Bible conference platform in North America once he called for costly discipleship and genuine spiritual revival. Like Old Testament prophets, he registered his disdain for money, and even urged his church governing board to pass over his name when it came time to review the budget and increase staff salaries.[4]

In truth, this frequently acerbic pastor cared little for the opinions of people when it came to what he should preach or write. A self-proclaimed "minor prophet," Tozer's ambition was to be Jeremiah, Amos, and John the Baptist to his generation. He knew his ministry required him to call the church out of its apathy and admiration for the world, and into the presence, knowledge, and worship of a Holy God.[5]

If the prophets of Hebrew history were unpopular, Tozer unflinchingly accepted a similar reception. If his preaching failed to attract large crowds, and if his books sold far fewer copies than many of his Christian contemporaries, he never registered concern. On the contrary, he knew his calling was to be faithful rather than successful by world standards. Antithetical to today's "market-driven" churches, Tozer's churches were places where the faithful gathered to worship God in community, learn from Scripture how God would have them live, and be sent out as heralds of the gospel of Jesus Christ to a fallen and hurting world.

Being a man who was steeped in the Holy Scriptures—a man whose soul was in a word, bibline, he probably never expected more than a remnant of Christians to take his writing and preaching seriously. What might have surprised him was the fact that the books he published in his lifetime continue to sell, and two of these, *The Pursuit of God* and *Knowledge of the Holy*, sell more now than when he was alive. Furthermore, many of his recorded sermons have been edited since his earthly passing, and many of these have been produced in book form. Like C. S. Lewis, Tozer had more books published subsequent to his death than when he lived.

If A. W. Tozer's voice needed to be heard in his lifetime, his messages are even more important today. The problems he confronted in the late twentieth century are still with us. Although he died nearly fifty years ago, we ignore his biblical messages at our peril.

◊   ◊   ◊   ◊   ◊   ◊   ◊   ◊   ◊

Although there are already two important biographies on A. W. Tozer: David J. Fant Jr., *A. W. Tozer: A Twentieth-Century Prophet* (1964) and James L. Snyder, *In Pursuit of God: The Life of A. W. Tozer* (1991), I have chosen to write another book for several reasons. First, some new resources are available since Fant and Snyder wrote their books. Oral history interviews have been conducted with hitherto overlooked or inaccessible people. Likewise some important correspondence has been discovered in recent years. Second, despite significant contributions of the earlier biographies in setting forth the details of Tozer's life, more remains to be revealed about the inner man. There are dimensions of A. W. Tozer that have eluded students of his life and ministry. As a result, this book attempts to reveal the inner life of this gifted and complex man who at once loved God passionately and deeply, sought to know Him with all his heart and mind and soul, yet found it quite difficult to relate with similar enthusiasm to his own immediate and extended family, or to the congregations God called him to oversee.

Third, inasmuch as Tozer has been dead for nearly half a century, we now have a vantage point of longer perspective. From this angle of vision we can evaluate his influence with more confidence. Fourth, early twenty-first-century Christians live in a culture that asks some different questions and wrestles with at least a few issues peculiar to our time and therefore not explored by earlier biographies. Tozer died before the high tide of the charismatic movement and the so-called Third Wave of the Spirit among Christians in the late 1980s,[6] but he has much to say to us in the midst of these profound changes. Indeed, his personal history can calm, comfort, and encourage us today.

Aiden W. Tozer probably never heard or employed a phrase popular today—spiritual formation. Nevertheless, he became magnificently obsessive about the shaping of the soul into Christlikeness. He shared this younger generation's suspicion of chronological snobbery, and he understood and lived a life of faith that drank deeply from the wells of wisdom preserved in the writings of the early church. Like numerous young adults of the early twenty-first century, Tozer wanted to be connected with the rich roots of historic Christianity, and like many of our younger contemporaries he instinctively knew that the Madison Avenue market-driven movement, with its disdain for the past and its concomitant worship of all things "new and improved," is deathly for Christians. He realized that anything "new" in Christianity would be moldy in a few years. He believed that preachers and teachers of "the faith which was *once* for all delivered to the saints" (Jude 3, emphasis added) must be dedicated to thoughtful contextualization, yes, but originality, no. Tozer would have joined theologian Thomas C. Oden in saying as a teacher of "the faith" that "I am dedicated to unoriginality. I am pledged to irrelevance if relevance means indebtedness to corrupt modernity."[7]

In the following chapters A. W. Tozer's life is unfolded chronologically, with emphasis placed on presenting and explaining the people, events, and sundry factors that awakened his soul and helped him mature spiritually. Tozer's continual response to the Holy Spirit's call is set forth along with evidence of how the Lord gifted him and then fashioned and refined his ministry.

It is instructive for people who desire to grow in Christ to learn lessons from the lives of saints who have finished well. With this aim in mind, I have been careful to reveal Mr. Tozer's imperfections as well as strengths because most individuals find hope by learning that God uses flawed people. Furthermore, I have attempted to show that Tozer, like all men and women whom God uses for His glory, learned from his mistakes rather than never making them. And it has been quite helpful to discover that the pathway of discipleship is not one of a smooth upward trajectory. On the contrary, Tozer, like all disciples, encountered fog and roadblocks along the way. The route of the Christian is never clearly laid out beforehand. Like Matthew the tax collector, the disciple is simply called out. He is not immediately told where he is going, but he knows the One who has called and promises to walk with him. Consequently the journey, although never easy, is joyous and fruitful. So it was with a boy who first heard the voice of God in western Pennsylvania.

2

"A Deep Strain of the Country"

Early Years in Rural Pennsylvania (1897–1912)

Anyone who hears God with clarity will be at least part loner. Times of solitude are required to open the Bible, pray, meditate on the Word, and then write down what God reveals. But to take the next step and walk away from the serenity of solitude, go out into the hustle and bustle of the marketplace, and speak God's words to indifferent and even hostile worldlings, demands courage and a God-tempered inner strength to withstand the inevitable verbal abuse and isolation.

Aiden Wilson Tozer possessed these attributes. His inner strength and temperament, in part, came out of the rugged environment of central Pennsylvania. He grew up in the foothills of the Allegheny Mountains, a place that demanded toughness for survival. In later years he said he grew up among a "frugal breed of men" for whom he had "only genuine respect and warm admiration." These people, Tozer wrote, wrestled "their bread from the Rocky soil," they "fell the might [trees] of the forest for commercial uses," and they raised cattle for milk, beef, and leather.[1]

Clearfield County, Tozer's birthplace, encompassed mostly small farms and a few villages and small towns that were service centers for farmers, loggers, tanners, and those who quarried the region's limestone deposits. The Tozer family's roots in the region go back to 1830. Gilbert S. Tozer, Aiden's grandfather, was born in England in 1810. He emigrated to America as a teenager and moved to upstate New York where the construction of the Erie Canal—the world-famous "ditch" that spanned the 363-mile stretch between Buffalo on Lake Erie and Albany on the Hudson River—required thousands of laborers who were looking for a good start in life. Gilbert Tozer married early, but his wife, Isabelle, died soon thereafter. Consequently, a combination of grief and high land prices caused him to move to Pennsylvania by age twenty. Although Tozer purchased land in Clearfield County, he primarily earned his living from lumbering. He cut down trees, trimmed logs, and fashioned them into rafts so they could be floated down the Susquehanna River or its branches to one of the several bustling lumber mills.

Twenty years after arriving in Clearfield County, Gilbert Tozer remarried. He managed to woo and win the hand of nineteen-year-old Margaret Weaver, a lass twenty years his junior. Margaret had grown up in Westmoreland County and never let anyone forget it. She boasted that her home county had better land and a more civilized environment. She bragged that she had been raised a Presbyterian. To her mind this was a badge of respectability because most folks in nineteenth-century America—particularly in the newly settled areas west of the Alleghenies—agreed that next to schools, the church was the most civilizing institution that could be brought to people hardened by climate and poverty, who pretty much epitomized the book of Judges in which everyone did what seemed right in his own eyes.

Margaret Weaver Tozer might have come from a region with more established churches than Clearfield County, and the soil might have been easier to farm, but she certainly did not hail from a soft-handed middle-class urban culture. On the contrary, her façade of pretense sometimes slipped, especially when she bragged of her skill with a scythe—a talent she learned from her father who, without any sons, put all seven daughters to work in fields each year at harvest time.[2]

In any case Margaret Weaver spent little time in the fields once she married Gilbert Tozer. She gave him eight healthy children in rapid succession, and most of her time was devoted to cooking and sewing for them. Although Gilbert preferred town life where he could be near lumber mills and his own gradually expanding mercantile and local political enterprises, he put his wife and growing family on the farm because he believed the farm environment would be best for their children. Soon after they were married he had built a house and small barn on his land and lived the rural life on weekends, but left his family and worked in town during the week.

Gilbert Tozer seems to have been a charming eccentric. He loved books, regularly read newspapers and journals, and carried reading materials to his farm family each weekend. Consequently, the locals dubbed him the "Gentleman Farmer," and admired him enough to elect him to the Clearfield County Board of Commissioners in 1872.

For years Margaret Tozer dutifully held hearth and home together as her husband commuted. The eight children all grew to adulthood, and the four sons helped expand the productivity of the farm. In 1878, when all the children except Jacob had married, tragedy hit the Tozer family. Gilbert and two other men were piloting a small log raft down the west branch of the Susquehanna near Wood Rock, a place where the rapids were strong and some dangerous falls lurked nearby. A larger raft accidentally overtook the smaller one, forcing Gilbert Tozer and his two coworkers into the rocks. The raft crashed, and Tozer hit the rocks and drowned. His two companions said their sixty-eight-year-old friend died the instant the raft broke apart.

Gilbert Tozer was hardly a young man when he died—especially by late nineteenth-century standards. But he was strong of mind and body, and no one expected him to leave Margaret a widow at age forty-eight. In any case, her life had taken an unexpected turn, and to make matters more difficult, despite all his enterprises and his image as "Gentleman Farmer," Gilbert Tozer was marginally poor, even for his times. Consequently, Mother Tozer needed help and she prevailed upon her son, Jacob, to stay at the farm, keep it going, and care for her.

Jacob Tozer faithfully remained on the farm with his mother. He eventually purchased the homestead from his mother and married a shy young woman, Prudence Jackson, from a nearby town. Prude, as everyone called her, came from a nonfarming family, and her father was a blacksmith and descendant of General Thomas "Stonewall" Jackson. Typical of these central Pennsylvania settlers, Prudence rose to the challenge of rural life and quickly became adept at milking cows, making butter and cheese, raising chickens, and trading some of her produce to local merchants for staples and cloth so that she could help feed and clothe her growing family. Jacob farmed the rocky soil and supplemented these yieldings with whatever he could bring home by hunting and fishing.

Eventually there were nine mouths to feed on the Tozer farm. Besides Grandmother Margaret Tozer and Jacob and Prude, six children came in rather rapid succession: Zene (1890), Essie (1893), Aiden Wilson (1897), Francis Mildred (1900), Margaret (1903), and Hugh (1905).[3]

The Tozer family was similar to other turn-of-the-century families in their part of Pennsylvania. They battled severe winters with harsh cold and lots of snow. Log and crude frame houses were drafty, and the only heat came from the fireplace, a wood-burning iron kitchen stove, and a cast-iron pot-bellied coal burner in a living room or parlor.

If Clearfield winters were difficult, summers could be equally challenging. It got hot in the foothills, and mosquitoes and other insects invaded the area and swarmed through open screenless windows as they were attracted by candles and oil lamps. The only respite came by dowsing the lights early, an act that not only helped solve the flying insect problem, but provided the sleep so necessary for the predawn wake-up call.

Prude Tozer coped well with the demands of rural living. Never a complainer, she washed, cooked, and sewed; with her brood of little ones she trod a well-worn path to the two-holer outhouse many times each day, in sunshine, moonlight, pitch blackness, rain, snow, or that ubiquitous, haunting fog that quietly invaded the hills almost every night.

From the perspective of almost sixty years, Aiden Wilson Tozer looked back with pride on his childhood and youth of marginal poverty where both nature and family demanded large helpings of hard work and determination. Rather than looking backward with self-pity, he saw his early life as a blessing. He nostalgically wrote that "being born in the foothills of the Alleghenies and spending my formative years in a region where few modern conveniences had penetrated, I happen to know what country life is at the grass roots."[4] In the prime of his ministry he reflected on the hardships and demands placed upon people who grew up on the rocky and hilly farms and in the small villages of middle America. He said: "Thank God that in the American bloodstream there still flows a deep strain of the country. From it we draw much of the courage, the simplicity, the dogged determination that have made us a great people. I fear for our nation if the time ever comes when the strength-of-the-hill-man is no longer ours."[5]

If Aiden Tozer manifested the strength and independence common to Central Pennsylvanians, he also bore witness to the specific influences of his immediate family and local community. Born on April 21, 1897, he had an older brother, Zene, several years his senior and almost like a second father to the other children. Zene worked hard on the farm, yet always had time to read and to help care for his siblings. Zene was energetic, intelligent, and inventive, and his sister Essie, three years his junior, talked more of him in later years than she spoke of her father. Besides carrying his sisters to school if the snow was too deep for them to walk, he amazed everyone with his inventiveness. His handmade wooden sled, complete with metal runners, not only awed the little ones, it gave them many hours of winter entertainment. No doubt Zene taught Aiden how to use his hands, but it is certain his love for reading and ideas, perhaps inherited from his grandfather Gilbert, inspired the younger brother to develop a positive view for things of the mind—a sharp contrast from the anti-intellectualism that often permeated turn-of-the-century rural communities.[6] Zene also encouraged Aiden to love the flora and fauna of Clearfield County. Zene became a father figure to

Aiden and the other children, but he moved to Akron, Ohio, for work in the tire factories at least a half decade before the whole family relocated there.

Father Jacob Tozer, or Jake as most people knew him, modeled aloofness and insensitivity. He seemed unwilling or incapable of demonstrating love or being personally intimate. Indeed, Father Jake seemed to have a huge appetite for hard work, but no stomach for thoughtfulness or joy. Essie, the oldest sister, said the only birthday party she could remember was her own nineteenth—and this is because some cousins came and took her off to their house for a surprise party. In fact, parties and celebrations were not a part of her youthful memories. At Christmas, for instance, Mother Prude would see to it that a perfect pine tree was found in the woods, brought home, and decorated. She made ornaments of popcorn and dressed herself up as Santa Claus to pass out her handmade gifts to each of the children. Father Tozer sat off to the side, not interfering but obviously uncomfortable with joyous festivities—he simply refused to take part.

Jacob Tozer not only eschewed celebrations, but the things his children remembered most about him were his discipline and devotion to hard work. He was not mean, but he was a strict disciplinarian. Life is hard, he maintained, and everyone must do their part to make a go of it.

The Tozer children also remembered that their father disliked holidays because they interfered with the hard work he demanded of everyone. Even so, Aiden commented on his father's sense of humor. One interesting aside on the humor, however, is that the stories his father told were invariably caustic ones that made fun of someone. For example, in 1957 A. W. Tozer recalled a story about an old farmer and his dog "that my father used to tell in Clearfield County. 'A farmer admitted he couldn't teach his dog anything. And he said he didn't want to learn. And the town bum, who happened to be sober enough at the moment, spat an arch of tobacco and amber and said, "Well, you gotta know more than your dog before you can learn him anything." '"[7]

Essie did not record her father's humor, but her recollection of the blue milk episode is rather telling:

The family at mealtimes always had fresh, creamy milk on the table. When Prude strained the milk in the morning, she used two small crocks in which she poured the milk—one crock for the noon meal, the other crock of milk for the evening meal. She kept them cool by placing them in running water from the spring (in the little wooden spring house). She also put crocks of milk from which she had skimmed the cream for butter churning in the springhouse and this milk would take on a faint bluish tint. One morning the child who was sent to fetch the table milk picked up the wrong crock in haste. Not long into the meal, however, father exclaimed suddenly in his sternest voice, "Who put this blue milk on the table? Get it out of my sight."

She remembered that the errant child ran out to the springhouse and quickly returned with the whole milk. "Father waited" until he returned. "When he [Father] spoke, the children listened. Discipline was tight on the farm, but the children were given much freedom to express themselves and have fun."[8]

In contrast to their father, Aiden remembered Mother Tozer as shy, beautiful, and humble. No matter what he and others saw in her, she felt she was so unattractive that for years she never wanted her picture taken.[9] No doubt those tender Christmas scenes stayed in his mind forever, but a day in 1936, when he was thirty-nine years old, touched the heart and soul of a little girl, and it tells us much about Tozer's tenderness toward his mother. Jane Kenney wrote that when she was ten years old she attended a Christian and Missionary Alliance Family Camp at Delta Lake, near Rome, New York. She said her birthday gift that year was an autograph book. "I set out to get everyone I knew to put an autograph in that book. . . . I was fearless in my quest. . . . *No* one was exempt" from being asked to sign the book and include a note. She recalled that even though she did not fully understand A. W. Tozer's messages, he was nevertheless "a target for a page in that . . . autograph book." One day she saw him alone, and approached him with pen in hand. He graciously took her book and "hastily wrote something on the page. . . . What Dr. Tozer did next stays in my memory as well. He reached out and gently touched my full head of dark auburn hair and said something to the effect that it reminded him of his mother's. Later, when I looked at what he wrote, he included a partial quote: 'Her price is above rubies' which I scarcely understood then."[10]

Grandmother Tozer's impact on Aiden and the other family members is difficult to judge. Family lore says she was a devout Presbyterian, but there is no evidence that she went to church once she married Jake Tozer. While the remoter areas of Clearfield County supported few full-time pastors, there were at least circuit-riding Methodist preachers in the area, and they managed to cover all of the little country churches at least every three or four weeks. But the Tozers did not attend church in Pennsylvania. Furthermore, A. W. Tozer himself said he was "converted by the grace of God when I was seventeen years old and there was no other Christian in my family . . . in the matter of faith I was completely alone."[11] Of course he lived in Akron, Ohio, by then, but so did Grandmother Tozer and the entire Tozer clan.

Grandmother might well have shared her faith with her family but apparently there were no conversions or much interest in Christianity from those in her range of influence. Perhaps she planted seeds and the fullness of time came in Ohio after 1912 or 1913. It is also possible that if she did witness for Jesus Christ to her clan, that no one could hear because of what they saw.

Prude and Jake's second child, Essie, recorded some markedly unattractive sides of the Tozer farm matriarch. Essie told her daughter that Grandmother Margaret could be critical of Prude's management of the house, especially her cooking. Grandmother's officiousness was more than irritating; on one occasion it was disastrous. It was a Saturday and Prude had gone into La Jose, the little town about a mile away, to sell eggs, milk, and butter with her eldest, Zene. Essie had been put in charge of the baking. Several loaves of bread were in the oven and the temperature was just right. Her instructions were to sit in front of the oven and as soon as the loaves were brown to remove them and then stick the remaining small loaf for which there had been no room into the oven. Essie "was dutifully and patiently waiting and watching in the hot summer kitchen, surrounded by the delicious aroma, when Grandma Tozer appeared."

Because Grandmother had originally owned the farmhouse and

still lived there with Jake and his family, she claimed the right to do what she wanted. Essie recalled that "she was strong willed and not especially kind as the matriarch and always had the last word in any discussion." Whether from impaired judgment or sheer determination to find fault with Prude's cooking, "she was convinced that the cooking stove was not sufficiently hot and began throwing pine chips into the blaze. The flames shot up the stovepipe and sparks flew out onto the roof . . . until the house was engulfed in fire."

Jake Tozer was working in the field several acres away from the house. Before he saw the fire and got to the scene, most of the damage was done. Essie remembered that the first thing Grandma did was "hasten to her first-floor bedroom . . . gathered an armful of her personal belongs and thrust them upon Essie, giving instructions to deposit them outside and away from the fire." Each time Essie returned to the house Grandma put more of her own belongings into Essie's arms "giving instructions to deposit them outside and away from the fire." Arlene recalled her mother, Essie's, story this way:

> Each time Mother returned, thinking to rescue some things of other members of the family she was handed another load of Grandma Tozer's belongings to carry outside. Essie had three lovely, new summer dresses that her mother, Prude, had made for her and a brand-new pair of shoes which she had never worn, but saved nothing of her own that day and, in fact, no one else's other than Grandma Tozer's possessions that awful day.

When Jake got to the house he immediately counted the children. Once he saw they were safe, he charged inside to remove a cache of money he had stashed away for a small building project. He did get the money but as he grabbed a large mirror in the parlor, the glass shattered into hundreds of pieces. He got out of the burning house unharmed but covered with soot.[12]

Aiden Tozer had reached his tenth birthday just two or three months before the fire. During the decade on the farm he learned numerous lessons, for better or worse, from parents and Grand-mother Tozer. Prude's parents lived far enough away that their influence was less marked, but Grandmother Jackson did get the lad to thinking about dreams. The Tozers remembered that Prude's mother, although neither generally religious nor particularly Christian, nevertheless fed the mystical side of her soul by analyzing her dreams. Long after her death, Aiden Tozer wrote off as bunk his grandmother's obsession with remembering her nightly dreams then interpreting them through the "Dream Book" she had somehow acquired. Even so, it is probable that Aiden had been influenced by her passion for dreams and their meaning inasmuch as several months before the fire he dreamed that the farmhouse had burned to the ground. According to Essie, "in his dream, he rescued his two younger sisters and his baby brother, Hughie." Consequently, when the house did catch fire, he followed "the same course of action as he had in that terrible dream; he took the three little ones down that road, over the hill and into the pasture." In later years Margaret "often told how she raised up several times to see the fierce fire but was promptly pushed down again by Aiden, in an effort to spare them all fright and hysteria."13

ⁱ ⁱ ⁱ ⁱ ⁱ ⁱ ⁱ ⁱ ⁱ

Aiden and his siblings were obviously shaped in profound ways by their parents, grandparents, and one another. And if the Tozers were not a particularly Christian family, there was another man whom they never met who nevertheless affected all six of the children. His name was William Holmes McGuffey.14 An exceptionally influential writer and educator, McGuffey published millions of copies of books. Americans bought one hundred million new copies of his school readers between 1850 and 1900. These were the textbooks used in the public schools throughout most of America until the twentieth century. Many one-room school houses like the little red school building the Tozer children attended used these books well into the 1910s and 1920s, especially in the rural areas of western Pennsylvania and all points to the west. There were six levels of readers: *McGuffey's First Eclectic Reader*, and five succeeding numbered works. Beginning in 1857 new readers were published and titled *McGuffey's New Eclectic Readers*.

Essie Tozer documented the fact that the *McGuffey's Reader* was the textbook used in Clearfield County Schools.[15] She did not tell us whether her school had the new readers or old, but that is not important. The contents, assembled, edited, and interpreted by McGuffey, were strikingly similar in both series of six volumes. To the point, whether it was the pre- or post-1857 edition, William Holmes McGuffey, an apostle of education, morality, and religion, produced books that he purposively shaped, as one historian phrased it, "to bolster Midwestern civilization against the dangers inherent in pioneering new frontiers. Since his Readers were directed to a supposedly classless society, they were all-inclusive in their appeal, and from them came a set of principles," which one authority claims "remained unchallenged in the minds of common people" until the early twentieth century.[16]

McGuffey's Readers, from which all six of the Tozer children learned to read, did much more than help youngsters build vocabulary and develop literary understanding. They promulgated a worldview that included Judeo-Christian values but not sectarian religion. The books celebrated rural values. Like the many philosophers of the Enlightenment, McGuffey taught that being next to nature put one nearer to goodness and godliness. Man learned important lessons for life from weather, rains, snowstorms, livestock, as well as small animals and plants. Man's immortality was stressed by McGuffey, and Jesus was presented as God, so He therefore stood above other philosophers such as Plato and Socrates, whose writings were quoted in the readers.

Good and evil were never ambiguous in *McGuffey's Reader* stories. Furthermore, boys and girls had the freedom to choose to obey and to be honest even in the smallest things. Invariably in these stories children who made the honest or generous choices were rewarded. The only losers were those who chose to lie, steal, cheat or be selfish. Orphans found homes because of virtuous moral choices, and wretchedly poor street urchins landed employment or gifts by doing the right thing. In *McGuffey's Readers* children were sometimes mischievous, but only immoral choices led to major vices or even jail. In these books children learned to honor and obey their parents, and mothers were especially singled out as important and worthy of praise. The readers contained little stories and poems to be memorized, and illustrations were copied on slates to teach writing, while reinforcing the principle that we always reap what we sow.

Lewis Atherton, a student of rural and small town life in turn-of-the-century America noted that *McGuffey's Reader*s taught that "School and home both paid obeisance to God's plan and God's law, for everything fell within His Master plan," From these readers children and youth from five or six years of age to middle teen years learned that "evidence of God's power and wisdom existed on every hand. McGuffey proved this with simple stories." Atherton paraphrased a story from the fourth reader this way:

> George Washington's father . . . secretly planted seeds in a design which spelled out George's name when they sprouted. Although George was surprised, he refused to accept his father's suggestion that chance explained the phenomenon. His father now admitted that he had planted the seeds to teach George a lesson, and urged the boy to look around him at God's planning on every hand. And thus, said McGuffey, driving home his point as usual, from that day George never doubted the existence of a God who was the creator and owner of all things.[17]

In a similar vein the fourth reader demonstrated that the problem of evil "in a universe governed by divine law was explained to school boys through simple stories. Everything happened for the best and every object had a purpose in the great plan of things." When two boys, for instance, were caught in a severe thunderstorm, one said he hated lightning because it is evil. But the wiser lad corrected his chum, explaining "that lightning was necessary to purify the air of bad vapors, a greater good thus offsetting a lesser evil." Atherton showed in the third reader that even the younger children met these morality themes through illustrations they could understand:

> An observant boy asked his father to help him cut down thorn bushes and thistles, which were snagging wool from the sides of

passing sheep. Since parents in *McGuffey's Reader*s were always wiser than children, the boy profited by taking his father's advice to wait until morning. In doing so, he discovered that birds used the wool to build their nests, and that God indeed was wise and good and had made everything for the best.[18]

Aiden Tozer and his siblings received a steady diet of McGuffey's worldview about God, church, parents and nature. Children educated from McGuffey's perspective—even five- to ten-year-olds—were taught about prayer, death, and immortality. *McGuffey's First Reader* presented the blessing of immortality:

> A little child who loves to pray,
> And read his Bible too,
> Shall rise above the sky one day,
> And sing as angels do;
> Shall live in Heaven, that world above,
> Where all is joy, and peace, and love.[19]

In the last analysis, all of the Tozer children learned to read and write through this series of six readers that revealed the universe to be God-centered, ordered, and personal. This was a marked difference from what their own children would gradually encounter in the public schools where the universe is presented as impersonal, man- and science-centered, and where submission to God and parents, as well as the efficacy of prayer, were either ignored or deliberately undermined.

⁊　⁊　⁊　⁊　⁊　⁊　⁊　⁊　⁊

To understand Aiden Tozer's spiritual and intellectual development, it is important to know that even though his family was relatively non-Christian, it was not anti-Christian. Furthermore, his formal schooling, although primitive by modern standards, was purposefully steeped in a Judeo-Christian worldview. Also, despite the fact that he left school at age fifteen, he was not educationally deprived. Although he never finished high school, this did not put him at a disadvantage with most of his contemporaries. Few finished eight grades, let alone twelve prior to World War I.

While much has been made of the fact that Tozer was academically disadvantaged as a child and youth, the truth is rather different. Unlike many young Americans of his generation, including city dwellers, his parents actually encouraged him to go to school. To be sure, he might have been a week or two late in starting the school year each September because he and Zene had to help winnow the harvests. Nevertheless, he was encouraged to further his education.[20]

It should also be noted that while he had only six readers to master in McGuffey's series, this does not mean that he only mastered the equivalent of grades one through six. On the contrary, these readers grew progressively challenging and by levels five and six they were rather sophisticated. What Aiden would have learned to read and discuss in *Readers Five* and *Six* was considerably more advanced, both morally and intellectually than what the typical urban public high-schooler reads in the early twenty-first century. One excerpt from the sixth reader illustrates the point:

> If you can induce a community to doubt the genuineness and authenticity of the Scriptures; to question the reality and obligations of religion; to hesitate, undeciding, whether there be any such thing as virtue or vice; whether there be an eternal state of retribution beyond the grave; or whether there exists any such being as God, you have broken down the barriers of moral virtue, and hoisted the floodgates of immorality and crime.[21]

In short, A. W. Tozer had inherited an exceptionally strong mind. His family encouraged him to go to school and as far back as his paternal grandfather there had been a love of reading. When his public schooling and *McGuffey's Readers* are added to this heritage, as well as who Essie recalled were some truly excellent women teachers, Aiden Tozer's mind was well-disciplined by the standards of his time. Consequently, he was prepared to begin reading on his own and thereby became one of the most thoughtful, self-taught, and well-educated Christian ministers of the middle twentieth century.

It is tempting to paint a picture of young Aiden Tozer that is beautifully sentimentalized like much Victorian art—especially when animals and children were the subjects. Such a picture would show young Aiden during the half decade after the fire, living in peace among the farm animals and wildlife, and resting in the teaching of William Holmes McGuffey's stories that all things are part of God's perfect plan, and that even what seems evil will certainly be offset by good. But such art would be far from reality because that kind of faith would have been an almost impossible stretch even for a lad of Aiden Tozer's intellect and maturity, given the hardships and challenges he and his family faced in the wake of the fire.

Evidence suggests that Aiden and most of his siblings were able to look back with the perspective of many years and see that God allowed that fire. Indeed, the Tozer family tragedy became a catalyst for good. But faith in all things working together for good for those who love God is a biblical truth—testified to by the mature saint—yet seen most clearly in retrospect and after the pain has healed.

The fire that came in 1907 when Aiden was ten years old and his oldest sibling, Zene, was seventeen, destroyed all but the foundation of the house. The inferno that consumed all the furniture and everyone's possessions except Grandmother Tozer's, also broke up the family. Parents and siblings with nowhere to live together were separated and lodged with neighbors and relatives miles away. Decades afterward the youngest girl, Margaret, remembered crying herself to sleep at night due to grief over separation from her mother. Although Zene and their father, with some assistance from little Aiden, worked as fast as they could, it took several months to build a new house.

As soon as the house was ready, the Tozer diaspora ended and the refugees made their pilgrimage home from houses of neighbors, friends, and extended family members. Although everyone was together again, something fundamental had changed. Even if it could not be fully understood, everyone knew the fire marked the end of an era. At minimum it revealed that the Tozer homestead was neither a permanent nor sacred Tozer abode. Indeed, the family had no sooner regrouped than Zene announced that he planned to leave. Since before the fire, he admitted, he had harbored a desire to move over to the fast growing Ohio city of Akron, where several factories were manufacturing rubber tires for those new-fangled automobiles that were predicted to eventually replace all horse-drawn vehicles.

Within a few months of the fire, Zene moved to Akron. As a result, the burden of the farming fell more heavily on Father Jacob, and he was forced to draft Aiden for work he was only marginally old enough to handle. These added burdens brought still more family fragmentation. Before the winter of 1907–1908, Jake Tozer suffered a nervous breakdown from the strain of it all. A doctor recommended hospitalization and rest to bring him out of his severe and almost paralyzing depression.

Quickly, more pressure to care for the family fell on the shoulders of Aiden who was not yet eleven years old. Evidently the youngster accepted his new responsibilities without complaining, but resolved to continue school despite his increased workload as he replaced both brother and father on the farm. Initially the new regime seemed manageable, inasmuch as farmwork was least demanding during the months of late autumn and winter. But spring came with its call for plowing and planting, and the weight of new responsibilities nearly buried the lad beneath the wheel.

Jake managed to come home in time to help plant the crops, but his respite from depression proved to be temporary. His breakdown of fall 1907 turned out to be only the first of a series of collapses and hospitalizations over the next five years.

All of this profoundly affected Aiden. Years later one of his sisters summed it up: "He was never a boy again."[22] Gone were the carefree hours of lazily listening to blue jays squawk and chickadees chatter. Leisure time for making live traps to capture groundhogs disappeared. Gone, too, were those precious episodes when Aiden could devote hours to hand-feeding and raising a three-eared lamb rejected by its mother.

The workload of the next few years did not destroy the lad's sensitivity to animals, but it did steal his leisure to be a Good Samaritan to hurting animals. Essie's recollection of young Aiden's care for one little pig provides a glimpse of the boy's bucolic past that the fire of 1907 stripped away:

> [Father] kept a few pigs on the farm. One sow in particular, gave birth to one more piglet than she could feed. The little runt was pushed aside by the other larger piglets and seldom got anything to eat. As usual, Aiden's tender heart was touched by this situation and he took pity on the little fellow and soon found the trusty bottle and nipple and fed him by hand. [We] children named him Mickey and he had the run of the barn and yard, too. When anyone spoke to him in greeting, he grunted twice, as in answering. When Mickey grew larger, Aiden would lie in the grass reading with his head on Mickey just as though the pet pig were a dog. Mickey just knew he was loved and he loved it.[23]

*   *   *   *   *   *   *   *   *

The young man who lost his boyhood with the rapidity that shattered his father's mental health, quickly picked up his responsibilities without complaints. Likewise his mother and older sister, Essie, took on much more work—and they did it with grace, as well. Nevertheless, by 1910 or 1911 it became obvious to Aiden, Essie, and their mother that maintaining the farm had become counterproductive, and downright destructive to everyone's well-being. Zene, too, joined the chorus of voices calling for change. Married now, and prospering in city life, Zene urged the family to join him in Akron. He made good wages in the B.F. Goodrich Company's rubber tire factory, and he expressed confidence that he could secure jobs there for Aiden and their father.

Only Grandmother Margaret stood alone in wanting to stay on the farm. Now in her early eighties, she had lived on this land since her marriage to Gilbert in 1850. To her mind it was disloyal to the Tozer family name to sell out and move to the city. Despite Grandmother's protests, Prude and Zene, along with Essie and Aiden, convinced Father Jake that the combination of farm labor, those regularly tiring trips to La Jose to sell milk, eggs, and butter, and the added stress of exhausting train rides to and from the hospital, were unwise to continue now that a more attractive alternative had become available.[24]

Therefore in 1912, when Aiden was fifteen, Zene rented his parents and siblings a large house in Akron. Good to his word, he also secured employment at B.F. Goodrich for his father and Aiden. By October the farm had been sold, belongings were packed, and Jake, Prude, Essie, Aiden, Mildred, Margaret, Hughie—and Grandma—boarded the train for Akron, Ohio.[25] Regardless of their hopes, none of them could have imagined the challenges and fortunes in their future.

"I Heard His Voice —Ever So Faintly"

Called to Surrender, Preach, and Marry (1912–1918)

In October, 1912, eight Tozers—ranging in ages from little Hughie, age seven, to Grandmother, age eighty-two—climbed aboard a westbound train for Akron, Ohio. Despite all the exciting stories the family had heard from Zene since he moved there five years earlier, not one of them had any clear understanding of the magnitude of change awaiting them in the eastern Ohio industrial city, the likes of which they had never seen.

To be sure, the Tozers were as ready for culture shock as about any rural family could be. They were intelligent, and for their times and the rural community they were leaving, they were well educated. Their ruggedness and individualism, hewn out of a demanding hill-country environment and shaped by chisels of personal hardship, further placed them in an advantageous position to fulfill the American dream. Nevertheless, what lay before them was like major social, cultural, and psychological surgery. The Tozers were, after all, provincial people.

When they looked inquiringly out the windows as the train snaked its way across two hundred miles of western Pennsylvania and eastern Ohio, most of them saw for the first time a striking change in geography. As the train steamed around the hills and out of the Allegheny foothills, the route straightened as the tracks pierced a straighter northwestwardly route. Gradually the Tozers could see a broader horizon and more level farmlands. Because it was October, most of the farms were barren with autumnal colors of dying leaves and tan remnants of the previous summer's crops. In some places ambitious farmers would already have plowed under the dead stalks, leaving evidence of black topsoil much richer and deeper then the Tozers tilled in Clearfield County.

If the Tozers peered out with wide-eyed fascination, so did most passengers who were heading to the burgeoning industrial cities of middle America. Fred Shannon in *The Farmer's Last Frontier* estimated that eighteen million Americans moved from rural areas during the period between 1860 and 1900. During the next two decades many millions more left the farms and small towns of rural America in search of a higher living standard in the cities of America's industrial revolution. The Tozers were part of this internal exodus from rural America that by the end of World War I left more than 50 percent of Americans in cities for the first time in the nation's history.[1]

The farm-to-city movement was only one part of the social upheavals of the late nineteenth and early twentieth centuries. Ten million immigrants stepped onto America's shores between the Civil War and 1890. Most of these newcomers were from northern and western Europe, so their presence was only slightly shocking to the rural Americans like the Tozers who had their roots in similar countries. Between 1890 and World War I, on the other hand, fifteen million newcomers streamed into the United States from southern and eastern Europe. This tidal wave of people, some of whom the Tozers would encounter in the railroad centers and industrial cities of Ohio, presented a high-powered shock to émigrés from rural America.

Such prodigious population shifts turned old cities like New York, Boston, and Philadelphia into giant metropolises. Newer cities such as Denver, Kansas City, Chicago, and Akron sprung up as if by magic and rapidly became regional urban centers, interconnected by railroads, in just a few years. People who populated cities like Akron experienced profound change—some of it good, some of it unattractive, and all of it disconcerting. On the plus side were employment opportunities and higher living standards for the new city dwellers. America's cities offered economic opportunities on a scale unprecedented anywhere in the world. With economic growth came higher incomes, and new political and social opportunities. On the negative side, however, crime rates rose in crowded environments, slums mushroomed, literacy declined, and conflict and confusion erupted when diverse ethnic groups competed for jobs and housing.[2]

The Tozers arrived in Akron when it was one of the fastest growing cities in the United States. Located thirty miles south of Cleveland and along the Ohio-Erie Canal, rubber industries attracted immigrants from Europe and the farms of America. Railroads quickly eclipsed the canal as the transportation arteries to move people and raw materials into the city, and manufactured goods in every direction outside. In 1912 when the Tozer family stepped off the train, Akron's population was approximately 80,000. Eight years later, in 1920, over 210,000 lived and labored within the city limits. In short, over twice as many people lived within the confines of Akron's city limits than in all of Clearfield County.[3]

The eight Tozers certainly suffered culture shock when they arrived, and nothing Zene could have told them would fully prepare them for their populous and bustling new home. On the other hand, they were much more fortunate then most newcomers. Zene and his wife met them, had a rather large house rented and prepared, and could teach them all the ins and outs of where to shop and how to get around. Furthermore, unlike many immigrants, they all spoke English.

Within a few days Zene had helped his father, Essie, and Aiden find employment. Jake went to work with Zene at B.F. Goodrich Tire and Rubber Company where he earned more money in a day than he ever did in a month on the farm. Essie secured work with Quaker Oats. Aiden, who always took the path less traveled, quickly grabbed a job on the Vicksburg and Pacific Railroad where he could explore more of America from the vantage point of a railroad passenger or "Chair Car." For a season this commission-only sales work, in which he peddled candy, peanuts, and books to passengers, suited his wanderlust. And, although there were always people around, he could be a loner in a crowd. In fact, he spent more time reading than selling. Consequently his life of reading and exploration from the relative isolation of a train car did not last long. He loathed approaching people and asking them to buy his wares. Indeed, most of his sales came from those who approached him. Therefore, within a few months, Aiden's sales career ended and he took night work at B.F. Goodrich where he earned an hourly wage performing the monotonous task of hand-cutting crude rubber into small pieces to be melted down for processing and eventual tire manufacturing.[4]

Aiden's job proved to be boring but it had some positive sides. While cutting rubber he could prop up a book of poetry and memorize verses. Likewise, he was earning enough money to help the family and still have a small amount of discretionary money for things of his own. Also, being away from farm life, no longer living on a train and working nights, ultimately provided Aiden with more free time than he had had in years. Always longing to learn, he enrolled in high school. But this pursuit of formal education was short-lived. He found the lessons and classroom boring, and he concluded he could learn more by reading books on his own.[5]

Aiden's informal education came from more than books and the industrial city; it also came from meeting a host of boarders who took two meals a day with the Tozer family beginning in spring 1913 when the family found what Essie described as "a real home again." In March, after five months in their first house on Laurel Street, several days of torrential rain caused a nearby pond to flood. Fearful of once again losing their house and belongings, they lodged with a generous woman who lived on higher ground. Although the water level never got higher than the porch, this was a warning signal to the once-burned twice-shy Tozers. They soon found a larger house—and this one they purchased with money from the sale of the farm. The new place was located on the eastern edge of Akron near the Goodyear Tire and Rubber Company plant. This was good for Jake who had already left Goodrich to work for Goodyear. Although other family members now had a longer streetcar commute, no one minded, especially since their new house proved to be quite commodious and comfortable, as well as being an unexpected means of additional income.

There were many single workingmen in the neighborhood who worked at Goodyear, and as more newcomers arrived, there were always demands for housing. Soon after the Tozers settled in, two men from rural West Virginia knocked on the door and asked for a room to rent. The Tozers did have a vacant room, so they rented it to these men who also inquired if they could take their meals with the family because, as they put it, restaurant food did not compare to home cooking. Prude had a soft heart for rural transplants, and she also needed the money. So she agreed to allow the tenants to join the family for two meals a day. Essie recalled that because the Tozer house provided "good cooking, others began to inquire about meals . . . [and] soon the house was overflowing with boarders at mealtime."[6]

The entire Tozer family did not eat with these workingmen. On the contrary, Prude protected her daughters and their privacy by hanging a large drape between the archway separating the living and dining rooms. She and the girls would cook and set out food in the dining room with privacy, while the men waited on the front porch and in the living room. When the meal was ready to eat, Prude or one of her daughters would call out "Soup's on!" Then they would part the drape and retire to the kitchen. Of course the women were not completely segregated from the men. One chap named John Jefferson got glimpses of Essie and she admitted that they both fell in love at first sight. After a period of courtship they were married and lived in an apartment near the Tozer home.[7]

It is likely that Aiden helped bring his sister and the boarder together because he liked to linger among the workers and take meals with them. He especially enjoyed listening to the talk of men from other states. Observing boarders became an important part of Aiden's education. As his biographer, James Snyder, put it, "These boarders afforded young Aiden opportunity to appraise people—a skill he quickly developed. In later life he assessed people almost instinctively, and with uncanny accuracy."[8]

The Tozer house did even more than provide income, give Aiden an informal school, and become the matchmaker for Essie; it became a signpost for Aiden's early religious life. Located in a section of Akron where several churches were built, the Tozers lived only a short walk from a Methodist Episcopal church that would become Aiden's first church home.

Aiden Tozer's first steps toward Grace Methodist Episcopal Church were preceded by some important events several weeks earlier. It was early in 1915, several months before his eighteenth birthday. He was walking alone and heard a street preacher proclaiming the Word of God. This encounter nudged him to wander into a nearby church. There, as Tozer remembered it, "I heard a man quoting from a text: 'Come unto me, all ye that labor and are heavy laden, and I will give you rest. Take my yoke upon you, and learn of me; for I am meek and lowly in heart; and ye shall find rest unto your souls.' Actually," he continued, "I was little better than a pagan but with only that kind of skimpy biblical background, I became greatly disturbed, for I began to feel and sense and acknowledge God's gracious Presence. I heard His Voice—ever so faintly. I discerned that there was a Light—ever so dimly." Looking back on this time of illumination he acknowledged that "I was still lost, but thank God, I was getting closer. The Lord Jesus knows that there are such among us today, of whom He says: 'Ye are not far from the Kingdom of God.'" Then a few days later, Tozer exclaimed, "Once again, walking on the street, I stopped to hear a man preaching at a corner, and he said to those listening: 'If you do not know how to pray, go home and get down and ask, "God, have mercy on me a sinner."' That's exactly what I did."[9]

Aiden Tozer gave his life to Christ Jesus all by himself in the family attic. And while this time of solitude was efficacious for salvation, his habit of being a loner could not sustain growth as a Christian. Years later Tozer looked back and admitted that he did not immediately move forward in his walk with Christ. On the contrary, although "I wish I had gone straight forward . . . I did not and most of us have not. We zigzag on our way to heaven in place of flying a straight course. I am sorry about this. I don't excuse it, but I try to understand it."[10]

Tozer never explained the causes of his early falling away. And if the evidence for causes is skimpy, it is likely that his loneliness was a contributing factor. "I was converted by the grace of God when I was seventeen years old and there was no other Christian in my home."[11] This is a difficult environment for mature people, and Tozer was still a teen. The breaking point came when Tozer met a boyhood chum from Clearfield County. Evidently a bit like Mark Twain's Huck Finn, this chap suggested that they leave work, family, and civilization behind and set out down the Ohio River on a raft. Set out they did, without as much as formal resignations from their jobs or thoughtful good-byes to families.

The Ohio River in the spring is high and currents are treacherous. Even experienced river men treated her with utmost respect. But eighteen-year-old Aiden and his boyhood friend were woefully unprepared for their journey. Despite some experience on the west branch of the Susquehanna River, these teenagers were no match for the demands of the Ohio River. They put off on a raft somewhere near the borders of Ohio, West Virginia, and Pennsylvania. Just a few hours into their southward journey the raft capsized and both boys nearly drowned.[12]

Aiden and his friend did not last as long on the Ohio River as Huck Finn did on the mighty Mississippi. But like the Missourian Huck, Aiden and his buddy got an education that ended some of their youthful innocence. The two Pennsylvanians slowly made their way back to Ohio. And, while we do not know the rest of the story for Aiden's friend, we do know that young Tozer eventually returned home from his adventure like the Prodigal Son. He made amends with his family, and quickly secured a new job with the Goodyear Company nearer home.

* * * * * * * * * *

The pilgrim's errant zigzags ended with the Ohio River episode, and he quickly determined to find Christian fellowship. He set his sights on Grace Methodist Episcopal Church for apparently no reason other than its proximity to home. In retrospect it seems evident that the Holy Spirit pointed Aiden there, but even this venture in Christian faith did not materialize without difficulties. Essie remembered that Aiden made his desire to go to church known to his mother, but admitted he "was too timid to go alone." Evidently no one wanted to accompany the new Christian, "so little Margaret, by then about ten years old, was outfitted and sent along." This, too, proved to be providential. "There was a godly, devout woman in the Methodist Church who took an interest in them. She had a young daughter of her own" and this became a natural point of connection between them.[13]

The mother-like care of this saint whose name has long been forgotten came at a crucial time. Tozer remembered these days as difficult. With no other Christian in the family, and with boarders packed in for morning and evening meals, "we had a house full of people at all times and yet, in the matter of my faith, I was completely alone. I must not leave the impression," he candidly recalled, "that I stood as nobly as Stephen in the book of Acts, but I did stand—and it was tough to stand alone. No one else wanted to go to church. No one wanted to pray at the table. No one wanted to read the Bible. But by the good grace of God," he continued, "I stood alone and I have always been able to thank God for the results." It did not happen quickly, but "my mother and father were both converted, as well as two of my sisters. A brother-in-law was converted before he died and several others came to know the Saviour."[14]

Aiden was nearing his nineteenth birthday when the woman who was trying to encourage him and Margaret in the faith, was pushed to leave the Methodist church because she was, to the mind of some of its members, a "fanatic." Consequently Aiden and Margaret kept one foot in the Methodist Church (where he met Ada Pfautz, who would one day be his wife) and one foot outside looking for the church where he felt he belonged. He did attend a nearby Christian Church on occasion, and the pastor there urged him to submit to baptism in obedience to Christ. Within a few months Tozer's former Methodist friend and her daughter led him and Margaret to the Locust Street Christian and Missionary Alliance Church, where her zeal for the Lord Jesus Christ was shared rather than discouraged. This saint who had been instrumental in getting Aiden into church life, became convinced that her newfound church was a special place—and one where Aiden would find the spiritual care she sensed he needed but was not finding. Aiden visited the Alliance Church. It, too, was fairly near his home. Immediately "several of the men took him under their wings and invited him to go to their street meetings . . . to give his testimony."[15]

The meandering young Christian had finally found a church home. Not only did he have a place where he truly enjoyed worshiping God, he found a pastor who loved and followed Christ. This shepherd quickly sensed that Aiden was a young man he should mentor. The pastor of the Locust Street Christian and Missionary Alliance Church was the Reverend Samuel M. Gerow. According to a young preacher who knew Gerow and met Tozer about 1919, this CMA leader was an "outstanding preacher and pastor" who came alongside promising young men and "taught them to witness and preach in the street, jail and [rescue] mission meetings."[16]

Gerow quickly saw in Tozer a young man of unusual intelligence and spiritual alertness, who was likewise purposive and eager to learn. The pastor took Tozer in tow, taught him how to study the Bible, find the plenary meaning of the text, and then preach and teach it with clarity and simplicity. He also taught his young disciple to humbly lean on the Lord through prayer. Gerow taught Tozer that prayer would illumine a text, prayer would prepare the hearts of those who listened to his messages, and prayer would unleash the Lord's power to bring in the Kingdom now and until Jesus returns. Gerow was the man who first taught Tozer the biblical and theological foundation of the Christian and Missionary Alliance: Christ as Savior, Sanctifier, Healer, and Coming King. This Christocentric underpinning of the CMA proved to be the water Tozer had been seeking to quench his thirsty soul. Gerow soon discovered that Tozer was an avid reader, so he introduced him to the works of CMA founder Albert B. Simpson. Next to the Bible, the books that most nourished Tozer's soul in the formative years were the ones written by Simpson. Especially important were *The Life of Prayer* and *The Holy Spirit.*

The personal mentorship of Gerow, the books of A. B. Simpson, and those early opportunities to give his testimony and preach evangelistic messages—all choreographed by the guidance of the Holy Spirit—enabled A. W. Tozer to hear a call to spend his life preaching about the Lord Jesus Christ.

It is tempting to present A. W. Tozer's life after conversion and call to preach in a neat, orderly pattern. The truth, however, was much more complicated. Like most new Christians, this infant believer found God's will one day at a time. There were many fits, starts, times of hesitation, and even confusion. He had no visions from the Lord and as he often said, "I heard His voice—ever so faintly."

With hindsight, God's guidance can be clearly seen. But, for this eager but immature Christian, there were many days of disconcerting uncertainty. The issue of church—or churches—is one striking example. Aiden and Margaret had been led to the Methodist Church by a woman they admired. But she also took leave of that church through ugly circumstances. Certainly this confused the new Christian. For more than a year he wandered from church to church. Amidst the journey he was led to a Christian Church where he was baptized.[17] When he finally met Samuel Gerow and clearly heard a call to preach under his helpful guidance, he still could not completely cut himself off from Grace Methodist Episcopal Church. In fact, he became a member in the Methodist Church and stayed there at least on a part-time basis, despite his ambivalence about that church and what had happened to his friend.

Any objective observer might have believed Aiden Wilson Tozer to be a confused young man who needed to grow up, make a choice, and settle in at one place to worship God and serve. But the Lord did not grant him permission to take leave of either Gerow or the Methodist Church because still more threads needed to be woven into the fabric of his life. Tozer would eventually throw his lot with Gerow and the Alliance, but he had to stay at Grace Methodist long enough to form a relationship with the Pfautz family.[18]

There is no way that Aiden W. Tozer could have had the fruitful ministry he had for more than forty years without his wife Ada Cecelia and her mother, Kate Browning Pfautz. Ada was born on

September 23, 1899 in a "semi-country area" near Marietta, Ohio.[19] Located on the left bank of the Ohio River across from West Virginia, the Pfautz farm was on rich soil and it lay near an established town with ample services and educational opportunities. Born in a log house, Ada was the seventh of eight children.

Ada's father, Jacob, descended from German and Swiss parents, and he was raised in the Dunkard Church. He left his church as a young man and consequently suffered disinheritance from his family. On his own, he moved to the Ohio River Valley and met Kate Browning whose family helped found the town of Marietta. Kate was an unusually well-educated woman for her time and in that region of the country. Her parents saw to it that all of their children received at least a high school education. Kate possessed a first-rate mind, did well in school, and developed a keen interest in poetry. A wide and deep reader, she published dozens of her own poems in local newspapers.[20]

Ada Cecelia Pfautz was apparently closer to her mother than to her father. Indeed, the letters she wrote in the 1970s in answer to questions about her life before marriage, are replete with reminiscences about her mother. Little, on the other hand, is said about her father. Ada remembered that "on the corner of the family farm [in Ohio] was a small Methodist Church where Mother and I attended as it was near and I gave my life and heart to the Lord during a revival meeting held by Mr. [William Edward] Biederwolf."

Soon after Ada's conversion, the family, like the Tozers, moved to Akron in search of a better life away from the hardships of unmechanized farming. Jacob found employment with Goodyear, and for a season the family lived in Goodyear Heights in a house their son John, who preceded them to Akron, was buying from the Goodyear Company. Located on Akron's far east side near the Tozers, Kate Pfautz and her daughter Ada could walk to Grace Methodist Episcopal Church.

Ada vividly recalled the Sunday she joined Grace Church. It seems that each new member was led forward, arm-in-arm by someone who was already a member. "On the Sunday I joined that Church [I first met Aiden Tozer]. He was an usher and it was he who took me to the front to join. I was a green country girl and was very

embarrassed to go with him and I said to a girl I was sitting with—
'that was worse than a wedding,' which he overheard."

At the time she was fifteen and he was slightly more than two
years her senior. Some weeks later "the Young People's Group was invited to a pleasant Sunday afternoon in the Church Parlor so I went
with my girlfriend and it was there I formally met Aiden Tozer." She
wrote, "Oh he was a handsome, clean-cut young man." After the
luncheon and Bible study Aiden walked Ada home. Ada said her
mother "had been praying that I would meet a Christian young man
and she was glad to meet him."

Mrs. Kate Pfautz took an immediate liking to the tall, slender
young man with a thick head of hair, large hands and feet, a deep
dimple in his chin, and piercingly clear eyes. She and Ada were both
delighted that thereafter he frequently called at their house. Ada said
her mother "prayed with him whenever he came to see me and I'm
sure [she] was a guiding star that led him to seek to know the Lord's
will for his life."[21]

Mrs. Pfautz soon became Aiden's spiritual mother. A Pentecostal
Methodist before the Methodists split apart over the doctrine of
spiritual gifts, she listened to him, prayed with him, and shared
books from her considerable library. Aiden himself testified to the
profound way the Lord used Kate Pfautz to instruct and encourage
him. One of his most powerful early experiences with the Holy
Spirit came during a prayer time with her. Many years later he recalled: "I was nineteen years old, earnestly in prayer, kneeling in the
front room of my mother-in-law's home, when I was baptized with a
mighty infusion of the Holy Ghost. I had been eager for God's will
and I had been up against almost all of the groups and 'isms' with
their formulas and theories and teachings." Continuing to describe
the significance of this time of blessing, he wrote:

> They had tried to beat me down. Some said I went too far; others
> said I had not gone far enough. But let me assure you that I
> know what God did for me and within me and that nothing on
> the outside now held any important meaning. In desperation,
> and in faith, I took that leap away from everything that was

unimportant to that which was most important—to be possessed
by the Spirit of the Living God!

Any tiny work that God has ever done through me and
through my ministry for Him dates back to that hour when I was
filled with the Spirit.[22]

Aiden Wilson Tozer had no doubt stayed in the Methodist Episcopal Church on Market Street in east Akron for many reasons. But
supremely important is that there he met a woman who was the first
person to lead him to the deeper life. She also encouraged him in his
early ministry and she gave her enthusiastic blessing to him when he
sought Ada's hand in marriage.

Ada Pfautz Tozer wrote "A. W. and I were married on April 26,
1918. He had been twenty-one for six days," and she was not yet
nineteen.[23] They had been courting for approximately three years.
Ada was an attractive young woman with lovely brown hair, elegant
eyebrows, and striking eyes that manifested her brilliant mind. Like
her mother, she was more than intelligent. She was well educated,
poised, and much more polished in speech and manners than Aiden.
Because of her advantages in being raised by a Spirit-filled mother,
she certainly manifested more spiritual maturity than her new husband. Looking back on their days of courtship, Ada wrote that
"Aiden being only a beginner in the faith and with little schooling,
[he] was dependent on the Lord entirely." With the Spirit's guidance
and anointing he went with a brother-in-law "some weeks to the hill
folks" of West Virginia. God blessed the preaching and "many
claimed to be saved or born again."[24] She candidly recalled that "his
English was very poor, pure Pennsylvanniaish [sic] and he said many
colloquial expressions of course." But those mountain "people did
not notice in W[est] Va."[25]

For two years before their marriage there were at least two
people who were diligently seeking to open doors for A. W. Tozer to
preach and teach. Not only was Samuel Gerow taking him to rescue
missions and street meetings, Mrs. Kate Pfautz was opening her

house for gatherings and bringing Aiden in to speak. Ada said, "My mother . . . would hold meetings whenever she could get a group together, and she was very delighted that I had found a Christian young man and she would get him to talk in a prayer meeting whenever she could get people."[26]

At least a year before the marriage Mrs. Pfautz raised money to start work for a church plant in Newton Heights, a new working-class suburb near Goodyear Heights. Aiden helped with this effort and did some of the preaching. Significantly this outreach was done with a team from Samuel Gerow's church, revealing that by 1917 Kate Pfautz was moving in the Christian and Missionary Alliance network where there was more serious commitment to home and foreign missions, as well as ministry in spiritual gifts, than she found in her home church on Market Street.[27]

* * * * * * * * *

By the time Ada and Aiden married in April 1918, an extraordinary fabric of purpose and beauty had been woven together out of what appeared to be the loose threads of several people's lives. In less than six years the lad who arrived in Akron from a farm in the foothills of the Alleghenies went from selling concessions on the Vicksburg and Pacific Railroad and wandering the streets without God to finding peace with Jesus Christ and hearing a call to preach. In little more than half a decade he found numerous opportunities to preach, and moved from isolation as a Christian to becoming part of two disparate church communities where he found mentors, friends, a spiritual mother, and a beautiful wife.

Soon after the young couple said their vows Aiden had so many opportunities to preach that he barely found time and energy to do his work at Goodyear. In fact, he and Ada both sensed that God might be calling him to full-time evangelistic work. God's leading seemed all the more clear when Aiden was invited to the hills of West Virginia to do an open-ended series of revivalistic meetings.

Consequently in late August Aiden resigned from Goodyear. Then the handsome and hopeful couple said good-bye to family and set out by rail to the rural towns surrounding Clarksburg, West

Virginia. The route was familiar to both of them. They went south to Marietta, Ohio where Ada had grown up, and then traveled another forty or fifty miles into West Virginia to the region where Aiden had preached a year earlier.

Early into the August meetings, Ada and Aiden Tozer learned once again that our ways are not God's ways. In the midst of a fruitful revival and enjoying the closest thing they had to a honeymoon trip, their little world fell in. Aiden received a notice to report for duty with the United States Army to do his part to support the American effort in World War I.

The notice was bad enough, but inasmuch as it had taken several days for his orders to be forwarded from Akron to a remote part of West Virginia, he was due to report to the Army the next day at Chillicothe, Ohio.

This surprise summons to military duty was only the first of a series of painful challenges awaiting the newlyweds.

4

"I Got My First Awful, Wonderful, Entrancing Vision of God"

Discovering God's Will (1918–1928)

In less than a week into what they hoped would be a belated honeymoon and newly launched evangelistic ministry, confusion, anger, and fear invaded the lives of the happy young couple. Having left gainful employment, as well as family and friends, Ada and Aiden set out in faith to do a series of revival meetings in Mount Pleasant, West Virginia. Having used up most of their money to purchase train tickets, they assumed that they were in God's will and trusted Him for future needs.

On September 4, 1918, about five days after they got to West Virginia, a letter mailed to Aiden in Akron finally caught up with him. The letter from the federal government required Tozer to report at an induction center in Akron on September 6, from where he would be taken to U.S. Army Camp Sherman at Chillicothe, Ohio, for basic training.

Fifty-five years later Ada Tozer remembered this staggering blow that left them stunned and confused. To be sure, the call to report to the Army was bad enough, but attending complications compounded their predicament. Being torn apart from each other was heart wrenching, but the Tozers had spent nearly all of their money to answer the call to West Virginia. Love offerings had not been collected yet, and the astounded couple had insufficient funds to get back to Akron. In a wealthy community, or even a large city, there would be people of means who could quickly stand in the gap. But rural West Virginia mountain people in 1918 were poor and most of them lived hand to mouth, day by day, just like the Tozers. Ada remembered that day this way:

> Suddenly he was ordered to be in Akron to embark for an Army Camp at Chillicothe, Ohio. We had no money to get home but the congregation somehow got enough together to send us. At first it appeared that I would be left there but I said I must go with him to my mother's. I was still only 18. I think he had to report the next morning.[1]

The dazed Tozers were driven from Mount Pleasant up to Clarksburg where they boarded a train for Ohio. Ada recalled that they spent a "miserable night," staying up all night on the train and in a station house at Kenowa, Ohio.[2] They arrived the next day at Akron—exhausted, hungry, and utterly puzzled about what they had assumed was God's call to enter evangelistic ministry. At the Baltimore and Ohio train station the heartsick pilgrims parted. Aiden dashed off to the induction center and a penniless Ada went to her mother's home where she was given room and board.[3]

While Ada lived with her family, helped out at the house with roomers and boarders, looked for work, and tried to sort out her disheveled emotions, Aiden was rushed to Camp Sherman, located outside of Chillicothe, Ohio, just about forty-five miles north of the Kentucky border.

Aiden W. Tozer was among the twenty-four million American men called to register for the draft during 1917 and 1918. War had been raging in Europe since August 1914, but America hoped to avoid the conflict. As early as May 1915 American neutrality became threatened when the Germans sank a British ship, *Lusitania*, where 128 Americans perished among the 1,198 people who died. Then the Secret Service uncovered several German espionage plots in the United States. These proved to be more than rumors and heightened imaginations of people who expected the worst. Indeed, explosions occurred at two locations in New Jersey—an arms depot and a foundry. Damage exceeded twenty-two million dollars.

Americans grew wrathful when the Zimmerman Note was intercepted and decoded. In this document exposed to the public on March 1, 1917, the Germans urged Mexico to attack our southern border in the event of war. By 1918, 2,810,000 men were drafted to strengthen the U.S. standing army that had been so small at 132,000 that it ranked seventeenth in the world. Although National Guard units added another 139,000 men, these were mostly poorly trained and equipped civilians who had hardly any federal supervision. Except for a large and modern Navy, and a well-trained fighting force of Marines (though they were scattered all over the globe at various U.S. possessions and areas of intervention), the United States was ill-prepared to enter the most devastating war in the history of the world.[4]

Aiden Tozer was one of those 2,810,000 draftees who were called up to become part of the American Expeditionary Force to help the British and French defeat the Germans. Formally inducted on September 6, 1918, this young man who thought he was called to full-time evangelistic ministry went through several weeks of basic training at Camp Sherman, and then stayed on to become a member of an artillery company. Private Tozer, serial number 3861239, had little time to untangle his twisted dreams and emotions. Assigned to a recruit barracks and later a barracks for artillery men, he lived among thousands of soldiers who were housed in two thousand crudely built wooden structures. Private Tozer worked from sunup to sundown, walking, running, eating dust, and sweating in heavy olive drab woolen uniforms. He ate as well, if not better, than he had on the farm growing up, and he picked up where he had been only a few years before in rural Pennsylvania—building up long-neglected muscles, working outdoors, and finding delight in shooting rifles on the practice range. He had done plenty of shooting on the farm, but the

1903 Springfield rifles issued to recruits were superior to any firearm he had ever seen in rural Pennsylvania.[5]

The intensity of wartime training left Tozer with no leave time to visit Ada. But he no sooner finished basic training and received an assignment to an artillery company, than the war ended and the men were quickly demobilized and sent home. On December 8, 1918, just three months after reporting for duty, Private Tozer's military life came to an end. With a few dollars pay in his pocket and some well-made new shoes, this Army veteran returned to Akron where he and Ada resumed life together and once again pondered God's will.

Ada recalled that she celebrated the Christmas holidays of 1918 with all her family. Aiden was "discharged just before Christmas and got home."[6] The Armistice was signed, fighting had ended in Europe, and the American economy looked stronger than it had in decades. For Aiden and Ada the initial storm of their marriage had passed, and they both agreed that despite the brief delay, God was still calling Aiden to preach.

Kate Pfautz, always her son-in-law's cheerleader, immediately went to work encouraging him in his call to minister. Ada remembered that as soon as Aiden got home from the Army, her mother stepped up as his advocate. Aiden "preached until February at Newton Heights, a small mission church my mother was instrumental in starting." Like her mother, the young bride exuded pride in her preacher husband: "I thought he was wonderful and I encouraged him all I could." She admitted "his English was very poor . . . and he said many colloquial expressions of course." Nevertheless, "those people did not notice."[7]

One of the reasons these little congregations were not offended by the inexperienced, unpolished, and country-mannered young preacher was that he was cut from the same forest as they were. Akron's booming factories were full of migrants from rural Pennsylvania, Ohio, Kentucky, West Virginia, and other surrounding states. These were his kind of people; he spoke their language, and he knew their habits and hardships. Indeed, he liked to tell them that he knew them and liked them because he came from similar stock. Jesus, he pointed out, knew people because He came and lived among them and He was made of flesh and blood and bones like all of us. Tozer enjoyed saying he was called to preach to ordinary folks from farms and hills because "I am just like you."[8]

What appealed to the new city dwellers likewise engaged the hearts and minds of people still living in small-town and rural America. Tozer made a profound impact in West Virginia when he preached there before his marriage. Also, the dear souls who dug deep for the money to send him and Ada back to Akron in September 1918 had been powerfully drawn to him after a very brief tent-meeting engagement.

Tozer's apparently supernatural ability to speak to the souls of ordinary folks did not escape the notice of the Christian and Missionary Alliance leadership. Pastor S. M. Gerow had been mentoring Tozer since 1916, taking him to street corners and small tent meetings to preach. Gerow celebrated his disciple's work in the little mission church started by Kate Pfautz, and he introduced Tozer to the Reverend F. Bertram Miller who had a small church in Kenton, Ohio.

Miller felt called to help young men get a start at preaching, so at Gerow's suggestion, he brought Tozer to Kenton in early 1919 to start an evangelistic meeting on the grounds of a public school. Tozer eagerly made the journey to Kenton, more than a hundred miles west of Akron, and worked effectively alongside Miller. Over fifty years later, Miller remembered his ministry time with Aiden Tozer. He had been tutored in preaching by S. M. Gerow, who, according to Miller, was "*the* outstanding preacher and pastor" in Ohio. Miller said that Tozer was not "a product of any college, Bible institute, nor seminary, but early on proved to be a great reader and student." Miller marveled that "even at the beginning, his pulpit manner was striking, but not extreme nor sensational. He was positive, biblical, and at times dynamic and convincing." Pastor Miller recalled that he and Tozer had "delightful prayer times and discussion." Tozer "believed all to be lost without a saving knowledge of our Lord Jesus Christ, and [he] preached for decisions." Tozer's "gestures were unique. His speaking demanded attention," even in this early season of his preaching career.[9]

No wonder then that the reputation of this able young preacher claimed the attention of one of the C&MA's most influential leaders, the Reverend Dr. H. M. Shuman. A highly respected preacher and teacher in his own right, Shuman served as district superintendent for the central region of the United States at the precise time a providential chain of events developed while Aiden Tozer was listening for a call.

The story of Tozer's call to the Christian and Missionary Alliance goes back to 1916 when Robert J. Cunningham, a former missionary to Africa, went to Clarksburg, West Virginia, to plant a church a few miles south of the little city. Like most Alliance preachers of that era, he was an able evangelist who pitched a tent, began attracting unchurched people, and led a number of souls to Christ. Within a few months a small, one-room building was erected and the Stonewood Christian and Missionary Alliance Church, just south of Clarksburg, opened its doors. In 1919 Pastor Cunningham received another call. Consequently, his little church plant needed a pastor. Both Shuman and Cunningham contacted Tozer and an invitation was extended for him to come down to Nutters Fort, West Virginia, and conduct a two-week series of evangelistic meetings. These meetings offered the Stonewood people and Tozer an opportunity to look over one another and hear God's leading about the open pastorate.[10]

* * * * * * * * *

When Cunningham and Shuman contacted Tozer in February 1919 and asked him to come to West Virginia for a two-week series of meetings, he found the Akron-based Army veteran working nights for a rubber company and preaching wherever he could by day. Tozer confessed that when he preached he felt God's pleasure. He knew deep inside that this was what he was born to do. Therefore, when this opportunity came, the young preacher sensed this to be God's will.[11]

This West Virginia call turned out to be a defining moment in the lives of both Aiden and Ada Tozer. Two streams were set in motion that flowed on for the next forty-five years. First, Aiden heard the call, answered with a resounding yes, and consequently embarked on a full-time preaching ministry career with the Christian and Missionary Alliance that would last until he died in 1963. The second stream also grew out of Tozer's reception of the call. He apparently said yes to Shuman and Cunningham before even talking with his wife. Failing to consult Ada was hurtful enough to her, but to make matters worse, he went to the West Virginia mountains without considering Ada's rather destitute situation. Fifty-nine years after this pivotal call to full-time pastoral ministry Ada revealed the depths of a hurt that would be repeated again and again over the years. To R. W. Battles she wrote: "Oh yes, he went with no regard about leaving me at Mother's and working."[12]

Within a few weeks, Ada grew tired of being second fiddle to Aiden's preaching. She said, "I wrote a post card alerting him to the fact I was going [to join him]." He might set her aside and become so consumed in his ministry that he evidently forgot he had a wife up in Akron, but Ada announced that "Mother Nature saw a different picture." She made preparations to join Aiden "as soon as I could get things arranged at home for my bother John to look in to check if there was food and other things" at her parents' house. "By then Mother and Dad were alone" and they were not as able to care for themselves, especially after "Mother had had several operations and was not able to carry groceries or do washing."[13]

⁕ ⁕ ⁕ ⁕ ⁕ ⁕ ⁕ ⁕ ⁕

Ada Cecelia Tozer stood an even five feet tall and weighed ninety-eight pounds when she was married. Thin, bright-eyed, and quite attractive in the long dresses that were stylish in the late 1910s and early 1920s, she packed up her few belongings and joined her husband soon after the Stonewood church called him as pastor in March 1919.[14] The church members put the young couple in a house. The parsonage was tiny but it had two splendid advantages. Aiden could walk to church and the newlyweds now had a house to themselves.

The faithful little congregation at the Stonewood Christian and Missionary Alliance Church typified the poverty of much of West Virginia in those years. In the Stonewood area people struggled for their sustenance by lumbering and laboring to maintain track beds for the railroads. There was also some coal mining in the region, but nothing paid much to these poorly educated West Virginians. Consequently, the Tozers received no regular salary. Instead, they were paid with fruit, vegetables, hunted game, and whatever love offerings could be raised. Ada learned to stretch the food and make clothes from remnant fabrics and ill-fitting hand-me-downs. As the Tozer's only daughter Rebecca analyzed it years later, this first church "set the family in a tenor of frugality that followed us" from then on.[15]

The Stonewood Church did not grow quickly, but neither did the local community. Nevertheless, Aiden Tozer was becoming known in the northern West Virginia area as a gifted young preacher. Therefore, by summer 1920 the Alliance placed their stamp of approval on him. The twenty-three-year-old minister appeared before the district leaders and passed their battery of questions. This, in addition to his ministry record and impressive grasp of doctrine and Scripture, opened the way for his ordination in the Christian and Missionary Alliance on August 18, 1920.

The solemn ceremony took place at an old campground, Beulah Beach Bible Conference Center, located a few miles west of Cleveland, Ohio. To A. W. Tozer, an increasingly serious and purposive minister of the gospel, this was no perfunctory event. Indeed, given his continuous reference over the years to the time of his ordination, it seems to have been more significant to him than any event in his life since conversion. To be sure, his conversion, his baptism in the Holy Spirit, his marriage, and his call to the Stonewood Church were all important. But his own references to the ordination enshrine it among the milestones in his Christian life. Immediately after the laying on of hands at the conclusion of the ordination, Tozer refused to linger for niceties, fellowship, and celebration. Instead he slipped away from everyone and found a place of solitude. There he prayed alone to the Lord who set him apart and called him to a preaching ministry.

The Reverend Tozer laid down a "Stone of Remembrance" for this sacred occasion. Although he could not recall the precise words he prayed once hands were laid upon him, charges were set forth, and promises made, he did soon after write out the essence of that prayer for others to read. No doubt hoping to encourage other men to take their ordination vows seriously forever, he wrote and published his "Prayer of a Minor Prophet" to commemorate this glorious day and continually remind himself gravely and solemnly of what he had done.

This is the text of his prayer as he wrote it sometime after his initial utterances before God on August 18, 1920:[16]

For Pastors Only
Prayer of a Minor Prophet

by

A. W. Tozer

This is the prayer of a man called to be a witness to the nations. This is what he said to his Lord on the day of his ordination. After the elders and ministers had prayed and laid their hands on him he withdrew to meet his Saviour in the secret place and in the silence, farther in than his well-meaning brethren could take him. And he said:

O Lord, I have heard Thy voice and was afraid. Thou hast called me to an awesome task in a grave and perilous hour. Thou are about to shake all nations and the earth and also heaven, that the things that cannot be shaken may remain. O Lord, our Lord, Thou has stopped to honor me to be Thy servant. No man takes this honor upon himself save he that is called of God as was Aaron. Thou has ordained me Thy messenger to them that are stubborn of heart and hard of hearing. They have rejected Thee, the Master, and it is not to be expected that they will receive me, the servant.

My God, I shall not waste time deploring my weakness nor my unfittedness for the work. The responsibility is not mine but Thine. Thou hast said, "I knew thee—I ordained thee—I sanctified thee," and Thou has also said, "Thou shalt go to all that I shall send thee, and whatsoever I command thee thou shalt speak." Who am I to argue with Thee or to call into question Thy sovereign choice? The decision is not mine but Thine. So be it, Lord. Thy will, not mine, be done.

Well do I know, Thou God of the prophets and the apostles, that as long as I honor Thee Thou wilt honor me. Help me therefore to take this solemn vow to honor Thee in all my future life and labors, whether by gain or by loss, by life or by death, and then to keep that vow unbroken while I live.

It is time, O God, for Thee to work, for the enemy has entered into Thy pastures and the sheep are torn and scattered. And false shepherds abound who deny the danger and laugh at the perils which surround Thy flock. The sheep are deceived by these hirelings and follow them with touching loyalty while the wolf closes in to kill and destroy. I beseech Thee, give me sharp eyes to detect the presence of the enemy; give me understanding to distinguish the false friend from the true. Give me vision to see and courage to report what I see faithfully. Make my voice so like Thine own that even the sick sheep will recognize it and follow Thee.

Lord Jesus, I come to Thee for spiritual preparation. Lay Thy hand upon me. Anoint me with the oil of the New Testament prophet. Forbid that I should become a religious scribe and thus lose my prophetic calling. Save me from the curse that lies dark across the face of the modern clergy, the curse of compromise, of imitation, of professionalism. Save me from the error of judging a church by its size, its popularity or the amount of its yearly offering. Help me to remember that I am a prophet; not a promoter, not a religious manager—but a prophet. Let me never become a slave to crowds. Heal my soul of carnal ambitions and deliver me from the itch for publicity. Save me from the bondage to things. Let me not waste my days puttering around the house. Lay Thy terror upon me, O God, and drive me to the place of prayer where I may wrestle with principalities and powers and the rulers of the darkness of this world. Deliver me from overeating and late sleeping. Teach me self-discipline that I may be a good soldier of Jesus Christ.

I accept hard work and small rewards in this life. I ask for no easy place. I shall try to be blind to the little ways that I could make my life easier. If others seek the smoother path I shall try to take the hard way without judging them too harshly. I shall expect opposition and try to take it quietly when it comes. Or if, as sometimes it falleth out to Thy servants, I shall have grateful gifts pressed upon me by Thy kindly people, stand by me then and save me from the blight that often follows. Teach me to use whatever I receive in such manner that it will not injure my soul nor diminish my spiritual power. And if in Thy permissive providence honor should come to me from Thy church, let me not forget in that hour that I am unworthy of the least of Thy mercies, and that if men knew me as intimately as I know myself they would withhold their honors or bestow them upon others more worthy to receive them.

And now, O Lord of heaven and earth, I consecrate my remaining days to Thee; let them be many or few, as Thou wilt. Let me stand before the great or minister to the poor and lowly; that choice is not mine, and I would not influence it if I could. I am Thy servant to do Thy will, and that will is sweeter to me than position or riches or fame and I choose it above all things on earth or in heaven.

Though I am chosen of Thee and honored by a high and holy calling, let me never forget that I am but a man of dust and ashes, a man with all the natural faults and passions that plague the race of men. I pray Thee therefore, my Lord and Redeemer, save me from myself and from all the injuries I may do myself while trying to be a blessing to others. Fill me with thy power by the Holy Spirit, and I will go in Thy strength and tell of Thy righteousness, even Thine only. I will spread abroad the message of redeeming love while my normal powers endure.

Then, dear Lord, when I am old and weary and too tired

to go on, have a place ready for me above, and make me to be numbered with Thy saints in glory everlasting. Amen.

* * * * * * * * *

Pastor A. W. Tozer served the little flock at the Stonewood Church for less than two years. Finally, in 1921 he accepted a call to pastor the Christian and Missionary Alliance Church in Toledo, Ohio. Then a few months later, denominational leaders urged him to take a church about fifty miles north at Morgantown, West Virginia. This church was larger than the ones he had pastored in West Virginia and Ohio, but even more significant to the Alliance leadership and Tozer himself was the fact that Morgantown was a growing city with unique potential to grow and make an impact on the entire region. Morgantown, in Monongalia County, is located on the northern rim of West Virginia, near the Pennsylvania state line. When the coalfields were exploited in that area in the late nineteenth century, and the Baltimore and Ohio Railroad completed a line there in 1886, the population grew rapidly. Morgantown quickly grew from a small town in the 1880s to a population of 2,000 by 1900, with 3,500 in the surrounding area. Annexations and growth enabled Morgantown to boast 9,000 people in 1910. When the Tozers came in the early 1920s, the population already exceeded 13,000, with prospects for much more rapid growth.

During the early 1920s, A. W. Tozer's reputation as an evangelist spread throughout West Virginia, eastern Pennsylvania, and all of Ohio. Under his ministry, the Morgantown Church experienced significant conversion growth as Tozer unflinchingly preached the gospel, lifted up Jesus Christ, and called people to genuine repentance, not just sorrow for their sins. Pastors and lay leaders throughout the three-state region implored Tozer to come and do weeklong revival meetings in their churches, and he frequently accepted these calls for special evangelistic services.

If Tozer's frequent acceptance of calls to travel and do the work of an evangelist led to many conversions and a widening of his reputation as a preacher, his itinerant work produced several negative effects. First of all, his marriage was put under great strain. In 1921,

1922, and 1924, Ada gave birth to three boys: Lowell, Forrest Leigh, and Aiden Wilson Jr. respectively. It is true that Ada wanted children. Indeed, she came from a family of eight children and often expressed to her sons that her biggest disappointment was not having more than the seven children.[17] But Aiden Sr. traveled a lot and left her with the work of keeping hearth and home together—a task that proved to be almost as difficult in Morgantown as it had been at the Stonewood Church. The love offerings were somewhat larger, to be sure, but the pastor was still paid, in part, by produce from his flock's gardens and little farms. Furthermore, Aiden apparently considered no one but himself when an out-of-town call came to preach. Once when the Tozer family happened to be visiting their relatives in Akron, and Aiden received a call to go out of town to preach, he not only left Ada with the children, but she had to figure out on her own how to find the money to get herself and the children back home to West Virginia.[18]

There is no evidence that Mrs. Tozer complained about her husband's absences from home during these early years of their marriage. She was always a faithful wife who evidently was proud of her husband and grateful that God anointed him and used him in such remarkable ways, especially given his lack of formal education and relative inexperence. Likewise, she lived in an era when married women—and especially Christian married women—were expected to serve their husbands and help free them to pursue their careers. If a husband happened to have a career doing full-time ministry, always dubbed "the Lord's work," a wife faithful to God and her husband dared not complain.

It is probable that Ada Tozer at once felt "called by God" to serve her husband, however difficult the task, and yet resented it as well. That this is likely the case can be seen in her candid letters to R. W. Battles in the 1970s, when he asked her to reminisce about the early years of marriage and ministry.[19] The tone and facts of these letters make it clear that for over a half century later she had carried deep hurts from Aiden's apparent ability to be a man with a single eye for ministry with only an occasional glance toward the concerns and needs of his wife.[20]

Besides the impact of this widening preaching ministry on the family, there was certainly an impact on the local church Tozer pastored. Neither of these West Virginia churches was prosperous enough to have assistant pastors. Therefore, when the pastor departed for other engagements, weekday needs were covered by Ada, laity, or simply left undone. And, if Tozer happened to be away on Sunday, the best that could be hoped for was that a visiting ordained pastor or licensed preacher could be found to fill the pulpit. Otherwise, a layman had to stand in the gap.

Americans were a hardy lot in the nineteenth and early twentieth centuries. If they were rural or small-town people, they were accustomed to having "circuit riders"—that is ordained or licensed preachers who rode a wide circuit of several counties. The little congregations felt fortunate to have a preacher once every two or three Sundays. Therefore, the rugged folk of West Virginia probably felt grateful to have a good preacher or pastor who was with them most of the time. Perhaps they thought little or nothing at all of his absences. Nevertheless, Tozer was already beginning a style of ministry in the early 1920s that he would pursue for the next forty years. And, while his churches all felt grateful to have him as their leader, people in larger cities increasingly expected a minister to perform a traditional pastor's role that included home and hospital visitation, and counseling sessions at the church office. Tozer did little of this classical pastoral care over the years, and in later decades it did not always go down well with some people in his Chicago church.

＊ ＊ ＊ ＊ ＊ ＊ ＊ ＊ ＊

The Tozers only lived in Morgantown for one year, making a total of nearly five years that they stayed in West Virginia, with a brief sojourn to Ohio. Years later the West Virginians expressed gratitude that God had sent the Tozers. To be sure, the churches had their ups and downs after Tozer's departure, but the two churches survived for at least a half century after Ada and Aiden had left, and some of the families that had been nurtured by Aiden's teaching and Ada's loving care were still active in those congregations well into the 1970s. The Christians who had first responded to the gospel under the young pastor-evangelist remained salt and light throughout the

Clarksburg and Morgantown regions for at least another generation. In brief, both Ada and Aiden had left indelible marks for good on the entire region.

Aiden and Ada's half decade in West Virginia shaped them as much as it influenced others. The couple bonded together through their genuine delight in their children. Even if they never became a couple who manifested demonstrative love to one another or their children, the children were indeed loved, nurtured, and raised on family devotions in their early years. Furthermore, the children neither witnessed ugly and angry fights between their parents nor was there even a hint of marital infidelity and the concomitant fear of separation, desertion, or divorce.[21]

On the other hand, Aiden's traveling schedule wounded Ada. Consequently, their marriage never knew the intimacy for which she so deeply longed. As painful as this reality became to Ada—and there is no evidence that Aiden ever longed for more than a surface relationship—she learned to cope. During the West Virginia years Ada found ways to put on a mask of contentment, and she channeled her affections to the children and needy families in the church.

During the West Virginia sojourn, Ada Tozer also developed a love for gardening. If her love for the outdoors and cultivation of fruits and vegetables began from need, it soon became a source of much joy. Of her children, Stanley especially remembered his mother's love for gardening, and she passed this avocation on to him.[22]

Over the years Aiden W. Tozer became famous for his delight in little children. Some of his admirers claimed that this showed how much like Jesus he had become. Perhaps, but most likely he learned to interact with little ones during the years that he and Ada raised three little boys in their tiny and crowded West Virginia parsonages. In any case, he may have enjoyed superficial interaction with children, but some of the Tozer boys said they experienced little, if any, true affection from their father. Certainly Aiden had no good role model for fathering. Two of his sons recalled that their father was so emotionally distant from his own father that they never heard him tell stories of the man, although he did share fond memories about his mother.[23]

The West Virginia and Ohio years brought more than three boys, family coping patterns, and opportunities to preach; they brought Aiden Tozer into a deeper mystical life with Jesus Christ. He recalled years later that "I can remember as a young Christian when I got my first awful, wonderful, entrancing vision of God." This happened several years subsequent to his profound experience with the Holy Spirit at his mother-in-law's house before marriage and soon after conversion. This second experience came "in West Virginia in the woods sitting on a log reading the Scriptures." He recalled one day when he was accompanied by a fellow evangelist. Always drawn to a more reclusive life, Tozer went out with a colleague but soon slipped off on his own: "I got up and wandered away to have prayer by myself." He said he had "been reading one of the driest passages imaginable from the Scriptures where Israel came out of Egypt and God arranged them into a diamond-shaped camp." God placed Levi in the center, Reuben in front, and Benjamin at the rear. With mounting ecstasy Tozer wrote:

> It was a diamond-shaped moving city with a flame of fire in the middle giving light. Suddenly it broke over me: God is a geometrician. He's an artist! When He laid out that city He laid it out skillfully, diamond-shaped with a plume in the middle, and it suddenly swept over me like a wave of the sea: how beautiful God is and how artistic and how poetic and how musical, and I worshipped God there under that tree all by myself. After that I began to love the old hymns and I have been a lover of the great hymns ever since.[24]

This early mystical experience in a West Virginia woods proved to be only the beginning—the first fruit of a personal and intimate relationship with God. The seed of mysticism had been planted in the house of Kate Pfautz during a time of Tozer's infilling of the Holy Spirit. It burst forth here several years later under a tree. The intimacy that A. W. Tozer could not give his wife or children, he began to experience with God alone, and this manifestation of "deep calling to deep" would grow more consuming in the years ahead.

One of Aiden Tozer's sons, Stanley, a pastor himself, maintained that his mother "had no inkling of his mystical side. She did not understand it and for better or worse, she was always a literalistic fundamentalist" who could neither sympathize, let alone empathize, with this side of her husband.[25]

❊ ❊ ❊ ❊ ❊ ❊ ❊ ❊ ❊

As A. W. Tozer began to travel more during his time in West Virginia, he became well acquainted with a number of full-time ministers. Two of these men in particular profoundly influenced him, but in strikingly different ways. One man, twenty-two years Tozer's senior, took him into his circle of ministers. He introduced the young West Virginia preacher to two of the most divisive spiritual issues of the first two decades of the twentieth century, and then tutored him from his own bitter experiences on how to be faithful to God without destroying his ministry. Fred Francis Bosworth grew up in Illinois in the late nineteenth century. Living some of his early years in the utopian Christian healing community, Zion, Illinois, Bosworth fell under the domineering and cultish influence of John Alexander Dowie, a native of Scotland who built a following of several thousand Americans through a highly publicized physical healing ministry. Dowie proved to be, at best, a man of questionable reliability. To be sure, many people claimed to have been healed from his prayer ministry, but he opposed the use of all medicines, incurred massive criticism from medical doctors, and led his community into financial collapse. Dowie died in 1907 at age sixty from complications following a stroke.[26]

F. F. Bosworth had been living in Zion and was exposed to both the good and the corrupt in Dowie's ministry. He was also there when Charles F. Parkham, one of the leaders of early twentieth-century American Pentecostalism, came to Zion and called people to seek a baptism of the Holy Spirit that would always be evidenced through speaking in tongues. This issue of tongues proved as divisive in Zion as it had been in almost every part of America where it spread during the early years of the twentieth century. Bosworth managed to distance himself from many of the battles, particularly because he was a devout Christian evangelist who refused to make either healing or tongues the center point of his ministry.[27]

When Tozer met Bosworth the American religious scene was ablaze with revivalism. Although D. L. Moody died in 1899, the man Moody discipled—R. A. Torrey—as well as many other evangelists, were holding fruitful meetings throughout the United States. Along with thousands of conversions, two other phenomena emerged as frequent companions to evangelism—the Christian ministry of healing and speaking in tongues. Few ministers in the evangelical Protestant world could ignore these doctrines, and there was little consensus on what the Bible teaches on these spiritual gifts for today. Responsible and gifted ministers stood both for and against these practices, and charlatans and corrupt men stood on both sides as well.

By the time Tozer met Bosworth, the Illinois evangelist was already a veteran of the wars over healing and tongues. Bosworth had to leave Zion and Dowie when he began speaking in tongues. Eventually he became a leader in the young Assemblies of God movement, but the leadership in this rapidly spreading brand of Pentecostalism pressured him out when he refused to teach that the initial evidence of Spirit baptism must be tongues. And while Bosworth himself spoke in tongues, he maintained that the Bible did not reveal tongues as the initial or necessary evidence for every Spirit-filled Christian.

Finally, Bosworth found his home in the Christian and Missionary Alliance. Still a strong advocate of the healing ministry, he delighted in A. B. Simpson's celebration of Christ as Healer, as well as Savior, Sanctifier, and Coming King. For Bosworth, the Alliance's "Four-fold Gospel" manifested the precise position he took and he believed it to be undergirded by Scripture. Furthermore, neither the Alliance founder, A. B. Simpson, nor any of his colleagues either urged or forbade people to speak in tongues. To the point, they maintained that the Bible did not prohibit tongues so neither would the Alliance. And because "Christ is the same yesterday, today, and forever," and inasmuch as healing is clearly set forth as one of the gifts given to the church, then the healing ministry would be encouraged and practiced, especially since Simpson himself had experienced a miraculous healing of his heart ailment in 1881. In fact, he ultimately wrote a widely read and markedly influential book, _The Discovery of Divine Healing._[28]

Bosworth, a wizened and battle-scarred warrior from years of battling both the Devil and other Christians, generously took Tozer into his counsel. He urged the still naïve and sorely undereducated young preacher to do the work of an evangelist, as this was indeed his calling and gifting, as evidenced by much fruit. He also urged Tozer to embrace the healing ministry, but to keep it as secondary to his evangelistic ministry. From the teaching of Scripture and from experience, Bosworth helped Tozer see that some ministers have a strong and primary healing gift while others are essentially teachers or preachers. He urged Tozer to be in fellowship with men who had healing gifts but not to feel pressured to do it all. D. L. Moody, for example, kept evangelism as his core ministry, but he ministered alongside other men such as A. B. Simpson, Dr. Charles Cullis, and A. J. Gordon, who wrote about and practiced the Christian ministry of healing. Moody even encouraged his brother-in-law, Fleming H. Revell, to publish Gordon's book on healing and Moody sent people to Simpson's New York church for healing prayer.[29]

Although Bosworth's primary ministry was evangelism, with a strong emphasis on healing, and despite his own practice of speaking and praying in tongues, he urged A. W. Tozer to preach the gospel, and celebrate and support those who truly had the Holy Spirit's gift of healing. Finally, Bosworth taught Tozer to respect the gift of tongues inasmuch as it is biblical. On the other hand, he reminded the West Virginian to keep this on the back burner and avoid his own mistakes of making this secondary and divisive doctrine anything even remotely close to front and center in his evangelistic and pastoral ministry.

By 1924, Tozer was ministering alongside his sometime mentor F. F. Bosworth. In Indianapolis and other cities of the upper middle west, each man conducted evangelistic meetings with other Alliance evangelists such as H. V. Cook, A. R. Greenwald, and Dr. H. M. Shuman. Bosworth's new book, _Christ the Healer_, came out in 1924, and it put in writing what the author preached—that Christ wants to reclaim souls and heal bodies today just as He did when He walked the roads of Galilee.[30]

* * * * * * * * *

Another Christian and Missionary Alliance evangelist and pastor who exerted a strong influence on the life and ministry of A. W. Tozer was Paul Daniel Rader. Eighteen years older than the Pennsylvania-born Tozer, Rader was as unlike Bosworth as can be imagined. Born in Denver, Colorado in 1879, Rader was raised in a mainline Christian home. His father was a Methodist minister who loved books and ideas, as well as ministry. At his father's insistence Paul attended high school, the Methodist-supported University of Denver, the University of Colorado, and the University of Puget Sound. After his university training, Rader served on staff at Hamline University in St. Paul, Minnesota. He entered the ministry soon thereafter, taking a Congregational Church in Boston and then one in Portland, Oregon. In 1908, feeling unfulfilled as a minister, he moved to New York City and took up secular employment. Within a few months he found the Christian and Missionary Alliance. The biblical preaching, teaching, and Spirit-filled ministry brought him to a point of profound spiritual awakening—something he had never experienced in all his years growing up a Methodist and then pastoring Congregational churches.

In 1911 Rader, after his John Wesley–like heartwarming experience, began street preaching and Bible teaching. Then in 1912 he took a position as assistant pastor to Pittsburgh's famous C&MA pastor, E. D. "Daddy" Whiteside. This anointed man with a gift for discipling younger men, helped Rader become a truly exceptional preacher and Bible teacher. Consequently Rader received a call to pastor Moody Church in Chicago, which he successfully did from 1915–1921. Rader was so prominent and widely respected that he was elected vice president of the C&MA soon after going to Chicago. Therefore, he divided his time between his Chicago church and the New York C&MA headquarters. In 1919 he was elected president of the Alliance, a post he held until 1924.[31]

Paul Rader had little time for or interest in either the healing ministry or gift of tongues. Actually, he avoided these doctrines. A man absolutely consumed with a call to do crusade evangelism, he advocated "union" meetings in every major city of America. He believed God called him to lead nondenominational evangelistic efforts where wooden tabernacles were built and protracted meetings (for weeks or even months) could be held, like those made famous by the early twentieth century's most renowned evangelist, Billy Sunday.[32]

Paul Rader left the Alliance presidency in 1925 so he could be devoted full-time to crusade evangelism and missionary ministry. Nevertheless, he had time to mentor other men. He worked closely with Oswald J. Smith who was ten years his junior. And he had a marked influence on Tozer who was young enough to be his son.

Where Bosworth taught Tozer balance in his attitude toward the sign gifts, and stoked his already burning fire to preach, Paul Rader, by example if nothing else, revealed to Tozer that he needed to study, read books, and build a personal library. It is doubtful that Aiden Tozer had ever met a city-bred man with such a keen mind who had been disciplined by as much formal education as Paul Rader.

For a man with less of A. W. Tozer's intelligence, discernment, and common sense, it would have been impossible to embrace two men like Bosworth and Rader who had such different pedigrees, experiences, ministry methods, and dispositions. Bosworth had little schooling and he was essentially a provincial man who had lived in Illinois for much of his life. He had belonged to a cult-like community and was theologically shaped by a new movement of Pentecostalism that found its following among the poor and uneducated. Rader, on the other hand, was by comparison, a man of privilege. University educated, a college athlete with experience as a boxer and football player, a product of an established and respected mainline denomination, and a cosmopolitan urban dweller who had lived on both coasts as well as the central Rocky Mountains and the land of a thousand lakes in Minnesota, Rader had fraternized with college and professional people of considerable means. In short, Rader stood in stark contrast to Bosworth—and to Tozer for that matter.

To Tozer's credit, he was thoughtful enough and humble enough to learn from both men. Consequently, both preachers helped shape him to become a man who was poised for ministry in urban America in the middle of the twentieth century.

＊　＊　＊　＊　＊　＊　＊　＊　＊

Thanks in large part to the preaching he did with F. F. Bosworth, Aiden Tozer caught the attention of all the C&MA church leaders in the upper middle west and Great Lakes regions. Tozer increasingly became recognized as a magnetic and captivating preacher, and with passion and authority he lifted up each of the elements of the C&MA's Four-fold Gospel. Tozer preached mostly on Christ as Savior and Sanctifier. If Tozer personally did not stress Christ as Healer, he conducted meetings in tandem with Bosworth where hundreds and even thousands experienced genuine physical healing. And if A. B. Simpson had heard the preacher out of West Virginia, he would have liked his messages and he would have been pleased that Tozer worked "Christ as Coming King" into every protracted series of meetings.

Tozer's popularity and the fruit of his ministry all dovetailed with the opening of a pastorate in a leading C&MA church in Indianapolis. In autumn 1924 the Reverend A. R. Greenwald, the highly successful pastor of the Indianapolis Church for nine years, discerned a call to full-time evangelistic ministry. His decision to leave pastoral ministry left a big gap in a church that for nearly a decade had experienced much conversion growth, raised up missionaries, and contributed large sums of money to support them. District Superintendent Shuman felt sad to lose Greenwald, but his spirits lifted when Tozer, who was highly recommended by Shuman to the Indianapolis Church board, responded affirmatively to the Indianapolis call.[33]

＊　＊　＊　＊　＊　＊　＊　＊　＊

There is no record of whether or not Aiden Tozer discussed the call to Indianapolis with Ada. In any case, she never registered any complaints. It is likely, however, that she celebrated the change. Not because she had no friends or meaningful service in Morgantown, but it must have been gratifying to this devoted mother of three little boys that for the first time since Aiden was called to ministry she could count on a regular salary. Ada Tozer never doubted that God would provide in West Virginia but it must have been reassuring for her to know that she now had enough money to buy groceries and would not always have to wait and plan meals around what the church family donated from their gardens, little farms, and hunting trips.

It is unlikely that Aiden ever thought of the strain that the poverty they experienced in West Virginia put on his young wife and mother of their children. On the contrary, over the years he was famous for saying he cared nothing about salaries and he even urged church boards of two of his churches not to give him raises.[34]

From the outset Tozer found the Indianapolis call exciting and rich with opportunities. Among the attractions was this church's commitment to missions and evangelism, which brought steady conversion growth. And, besides the joy of pasturing a healthy and growing church, where he preached his first sermon as pastor on December 7, 1924, Tozer was charged by the church to become the editor of a monthly church newspaper called *The Light of Life*. In this four-page periodical Tozer's sermons would be published and spread throughout the city, and the little paper would also offer articles on exciting ministries, advertise forthcoming evangelistic meetings, and publish small pieces by his fellow workers such as F. F. Bosworth and Paul Rader. Likewise, Tozer would fill out the columns with rich little feasts from previously published books by C&MA founder A. B. Simpson, as well as Protestant saints such as George Mueller and A. A. Bonar.[35]

The vibrant church, called the Gospel Tabernacle and located in the heart of the city on Park Avenue and 10th Street, plus this little religious paper edited there, served as strong magnets to get Tozer to Indianapolis, but there were other inducements too. Indianapolis— in part because of the exciting church ministry Greenwald had established—had become a hub of evangelistic, healing, and other

C&MA–related meetings. Consequently, it was an exciting place where church leaders gathered to share visions and encourage one another to be purposive about building the Kingdom of God. Added to these attractions, it was not lost on A. W. Tozer that Indianapolis had a splendid public library and some first-rate second-hand bookshops. Always eager to learn and read, and encouraged in this vein by Paul Rader, Tozer the student had an opportunity to discipline his mind and soul in ways that it would have been difficult to do in Morgantown in the 1920s.

*   *   *   *   *   *   *   *   *

Always a reflective man, A. W. Tozer must have pondered this splendid opportunity in Indianapolis with wonder and thanksgiving. In less than a decade God had placed people in his life who had been instrumental in preparing him for a ministry with a widening range of influence. Only nine years earlier Tozer had heard the Gospel from a street preacher and responded by asking the Lord for mercy. Three years later he married the woman who would give him seven children and patiently assist him in a demanding preaching and writing ministry. From Ada's mother he first learned about the baptism and power of the Holy Spirit, and thereby gained his first glimpses into biblical Christian mysticism. From Pastor S. M. Gerow he received his initial lessons in preaching. Bosworth then introduced him to a biblical and fruitful healing ministry, as well as to a balanced and sober view of all the sign gifts, including tongues. Paul Rader fueled the fire for learning that had started on the Pennsylvania farm, and through access to a good public library and bookshops in Indianapolis he began to discipline his strong but untrained mind on philosophy, history, the sciences, and poetry.

The Tozers remained in Indianapolis until 1928. During these three years Aiden honed his preaching skills, saw numerous souls repent and turn to Christ for salvation, and witnessed powerful works of physical and spiritual healing. Furthermore, his work on *The Light of Life* provided valuable experience as a writer and editor.

Indianapolis offered more than ministry experience, in this dynamic and growing city Ada Pfautz helped inflate the census by giving birth to two more sons, Wendell and Rolland.[36] Despite an even larger family to feed, the regular church salary contributed some relief to the cost of feeding hungry mouths. Nevertheless, some changes during the Indianapolis years drove a wider wedge between Ada and Aiden. Ada's pregnancy with boy number four (Wendell) went well but boy number five (Rolland) caused her weight to balloon from 98 to 132 pounds. She could never lose this weight and, at least according to Rolland, she blamed him for the permanent loss of her trim figure.[37]

The stress of change, and the general strain of having four boys younger than eight years of age were challenging enough. But Aiden traveled as much after the move to Indiana as he had when they lived in West Virginia. Being absent in body was bad enough, but the Indianapolis Public Library offered this intellectually hungry man an educational feast of gigantic proportions. With a burning desire to learn and a keen sense of educational inadequacy, Tozer began to devote long hours to reading. He not only read a lot, his mind was preoccupied when he was home, as he continually sorted out ideas and wrote articles in his mind when he could not be alone to put them on paper.

By early 1928 the Tozers had a routine. Aiden found his fulfillment in reading, preparing sermons, preaching, and weaving travel into his demanding and exciting schedule, while Ada learned to cope. She dutifully washed, ironed, cooked, and cared for the little ones, and developed the art of shoving her pain deep down inside. Most of the time she pretended there was no hurt, but when it erupted, she usually blamed herself for not being godly enough to conquer her longing for intimacy from an emotionally aloof husband.

As Aiden's energies were poured into study and ministry, Ada's attentions and strength were channeled toward the boys. Life was far from perfect, to be sure, but it was stable and familiar. Consequently, neither she nor Aiden was prepared for the momentous change that was about to occur.

"It May Be a Good Thing I Never Went to Seminary"

The Chicago Years (1928–1941)

M r. J. Francis Chase, an urbane, sophisticated, and well-educated Chicago commercial artist, met Aiden Tozer face-to-face for the first time in August 1928. The afternoon encounter became the first of countless meetings between two men who were destined to become closest of friends. Chase, according to those who knew him, stood out among his contemporaries.[1] He had an absolutely brilliant mind tempered by humility formed through a singularly strong and personal acquaintance with Jesus Christ through the Holy Spirit. Chase's spirituality was formed by Scripture and radical obedience to God's commands, but it was also enlivened through a mystical relationship with Jesus Christ whom Chase faithfully served and believed to be as alive and present today as when He walked the dusty roads of Galilee.

More than forty years after their first meeting, Francis Chase recalled recognizing a sacred anointing on Tozer. Chase, who embraced a robust view of the Holy Spirit, maintained that "I've heard people pray and speak at times—way beyond themselves—Paul said this is the best Gift, and so it is [and] would to God this would come to hundreds of our men."[2] To Chase's mind this was the only reasonable explanation of Tozer's powerful pulpit presence when he spoke to the congregation of Chicago's Southside Tabernacle in late summer 1928.

R. R. Brown (always known as R. R. Brown), who served as superintendent of the western district of the C&MA, arranged for Tozer to speak at Chicago's Southside Alliance Tabernacle. Brown had earned a well-deserved reputation as an intelligent and balanced, yet impassioned preacher with a heart for missions and evangelism. Along with Paul Rader, Tozer's mentor who became president of the C&MA, Brown urged Alliance leadership to broaden their horizons beyond the northeastern region of the United States where it was first organized by founder A. B. Simpson. Rader had tapped Brown to be first superintendent of the western district; so Brown gathered a group of young men to start a congregation in Chicago. They officially organized in 1922 and the faithful and energetic Brown served as the first pastor. Within a few months a permanent pastor was appointed, and by summer 1928 three men had followed Brown in the Southside pulpit, with each pastor staying about two years.[3]

Three pastors in six years was by no means evidence of a sick congregation. Turnover every two or three years was not uncommon in the early twentieth century. Indeed, the early Methodists, among other traditions, argued that regular turnover was healthy inasmuch as it kept the congregations from developing a dependence on one man. In fact, the Southside Tabernacle seemed quite healthy in 1928. They had a congregation of about eighty adults and, as Tozer's biographer James L. Snyder explained, this was "at the time a sizeable gathering for the Alliance." Actually, the Chicago congregation had more than a solid congregation; the people had already purchased a piece of property—complete with a large garage—that they renovated into a tabernacle complete with restrooms, education facilities, and a small pastor's study.[4]

Ample facilities and strong congregation notwithstanding, Southside's pastor, Joseph Hogue, moved on in summer 1928. Superintendent Brown moved quickly to fill his place because part of his vision for the western district was to have a strong church in Chicago. The Windy City, after all, was more than the dominant regional metropolis—it was one of America's fastest growing cities. Already the railroad center of the United States, Chicago had grown by 1928 to over 3,300,000 people in less than a century. An extensive rail network, complemented by visionary entrepreneurs, enabled Chicago to become an economic hub for gathering, processing, and manufacturing almost everything from grain and meat to lumber, coal, steel, and cement.

If Chicago had become the economic heartbeat for much of America, men like R. R. Brown carried on evangelist Dwight L. Moody's vision to make Chicago an ever-growing center for the promulgation of the gospel. Because it had evangelical and fundamentalist educational institutions such as Wheaton College and Moody Bible Institute, men like Rader and Brown saw Chicago as strategically poised to equip upcoming generations for home and foreign evangelism and missions.[5]

Reverend Brown had heard Aiden Tozer speak on several occasions and despite Tozer's relatively young age—he was only thirty-one years old—the superintendent agreed with Paul Rader that Tozer towered over other men and was proving to be one of the most energetic, passionate, and hopeful men in the C&MA. Added to these voices of praise, the word had spread in the Chicago church that several people were already urging the leaders to see if the Indianapolis preacher could be persuaded to move to Chicago.[6]

Consequently Brown wrote and asked Tozer if he had any interest in pastoring the Tabernacle in Chicago. Tozer responded with a polite no. But Brown persisted. He wrote a second time. Again Tozer said no. Despite two negative replies, Brown once again implored the Indianapolis pastor to at least come out to Chicago, meet the leaders, and speak to their congregation.

Perhaps out of deference to his superintendent, Tozer agreed to preach in Chicago on one Sunday in mid-August, but he made it clear that the ministry was going well in Indianapolis, and that he and his family were settled. They loved the people in Indiana and felt no leading to move. Nevertheless, Tozer put his preferences aside and arrived in Chicago in time to preach at 3:00 p.m. on Sunday, August 12. (In those days Alliance churches only met on Sunday afternoons and evenings.) [7]

Francis Chase officiated the service and he led the team of laymen and welcomed Tozer. Chase remembered that it was an extremely hot afternoon and Tozer arrived just a few minutes before 3:00. Chase introduced himself to the preacher and explained that he would preside at the service and that all Tozer needed to do was speak after he was introduced. Chase recalled Tozer's appearance this way: "He was slight with plenty of hair, and certainly not a fashion plate, as we say. His black tie was about one and a quarter inch in width. His shoes were even then outmoded, high-tops with hooks partway up." To put a fine point on it, "A. W. Tozer did not make an imposing appearance." [8]

Tozer's appearance removed any doubt there might have been that he was a rural-bred man who had lived much of his adult life among West Virginia hill people. His preaching quickly washed away any scent of urban snobbery that tainted the manners of some city preachers, and when Tozer stepped up to the pulpit he dismissed customary niceties about being honored to speak and ignored the habit of telling a joke or humorous story just to grab the congregation's attention. Instead, Tozer simply announced his topic, read from Hebrews 11, and then proceeded to preach.

Tozer's presence magnetically attracted attention. With a stunningly fresh voice, he opened the text and led people into the presence of God. Amid hushed conversations after the service, the congregation broke up into little clusters—still staggering from the spiritual power that thrust their minds and hearts to the Lord Jesus Christ. To a person, they agreed that a most singular man with a sacred anointing had entered their midst. His message was simple, yet eloquent. God was glorified and the people were blessed.

At 7:30 p.m. everyone who possibly could returned to hear Tozer's second message. Many of them brought friends and acquaintances along to hear the new voice God placed in their midst from the neighboring state of Indiana. Once again, without preliminaries or verbal decorations, the Indianapolis pastor opened the Bible and preached on "The Resurrection of the Dead." As before, the listeners were either driven to their knees in confession or lifted up to the heavens in praise. After the benediction a murmur could be heard among the regular members: "Don't let him get away."

Forty-six years later Francis Chase said he could recall as if it were yesterday the electricity in the air. Everyone present that night sensed a Presence in their midst greater than Tozer or themselves. An almost palpable sense of expectation filled the Southside Alliance Tabernacle.[9]

When Tozer met briefly with the members of the board after the service, he spoke with a twinkle in his eyes, "I do not choose to run." Everyone present that night knew that America's beloved President Calvin Coolidge had conveyed those precise words ten days earlier to a stunned crowd of reporters at a White House press conference. Coolidge, it turned out, meant what he said and refused to seek re-election to the White House in November. Tozer, on the other hand, left the door of hope slightly ajar when he said he loved the church in Indianapolis but agreed to return to Chicago a few weeks later to conduct a three-day preaching series.

⁹　⁹　⁹　⁹　⁹　⁹　⁹　⁹　⁹

By early October Chicago's hot weather had passed, but the desire to have Aiden W. Tozer as the Southside pastor had grown more intense. His three-day series went even better than the August Sunday sermons. Furthermore, Tozer found Chicago to his liking. There were many more secondhand bookshops in the Windy City than in Indianapolis, and the Chicago Public Library rivaled any book repository in the nation with the exception of the New York Public Library and the Library of Congress in Washington DC. In addition, Chicago's railway network greatly simplified travel to any place Tozer might be asked to speak.

Two other worldly factors played into Tozer's changing attitude about a move to Illinois. First, he liked Southside Alliance lay leader Francis Chase as well, if not better, than any man he had ever met. From their initial meeting in August, both men sensed a kinship. Each man knew he had found a special friend. Second, when Tozer explained that he would only come to Chicago if he could be more of a preaching and teaching minister than a visitation and counseling minister, the board agreed.

The final factor that caused Tozer to accept Chicago's call was the nudging of the Holy Spirit. From the time Tozer had received Dr. R. R. Brown's third letter, he had an inner sense of illumination. This light grew brighter when he went to Chicago in August—even when he announced, "I do not choose to run." Although still reluctant to sever his ties to the congregation in Indianapolis, he increasingly saw Chicago with new eyes. Finally, after the three-day stay in October, he had enough light to see the way.

Soon after Tozer's October appearance at the Chicago garage-turned-tabernacle, the little group of Alliance regular attenders received a succinctly worded postcard from Francis Chase that proved to be much like their plain-spoken pastor elect:

He was elected, has accepted, and will be here on November 8, 1928, and he is called Rev. A. W. Tozer, the man from Indianapolis.[10]

⁕   ⁕   ⁕   ⁕   ⁕   ⁕   ⁕   ⁕   ⁕

In early November Ada and Aiden loaded the five boys and everyone's clothing into a 1925 Oakland—a gift from the Indianapolis church—that was about as fashionable as Aiden's high-top buttoned shoes. The family belongings that would not fit inside the rickety sedan were strapped on the top and tied to the back end. The spirits of all seven travelers were nearly as low as the weighted-down automobile's springs, but the mood—at least for the driver of the family—shifted appreciably after a few miles on the road. Tozer later confessed to Francis Chase that Ada was terribly sad as they left Indianapolis. Tozer himself left burdened of spirit and quite frankly wondered if he had been mistaken to accept the Chicago offer. But the guidance to go west soon proved to be providential. Tozer said, "As soon as I passed the city limits of Indianapolis I had a favorable earnest in my spirit concerning my decision. There swept over my soul a sweet peace. I knew that I was in the will of God."[11]

The Tozers lumbered for hours in a northwesterly direction across Indiana. The highway was flat and narrow with only two lanes. The creaking Oakland, with a burden of weight it was never designed to carry, did not move fast, but it did get the seven Tozers to their new home without a flat tire or hint of mechanical failure.

It is tempting to think Aiden Tozer made a bargain with the creaking and straining Oakland: "Get us to Chicago and we will let you rest," because the Oakland was unloaded and parked in a garage behind the house, and except for one time it never came out of its hideaway. Ada did not drive until very late in life after her husband's death, and Aiden always found Chicago traffic absolutely intimidating. After a single-car accident with one of the thousands of trees that lined the residential streets on the southside of Chicago a day or two after moving to the Windy City, the Alliance pastor left the car in the garage. He took public transportation to church and downtown Chicago, or he hitched rides with church members who were always delighted to take the Tozers anywhere they needed to go.[12]

The Chicago Alliance Church rented a parsonage for their new pastor and his family at 10735 Prospect on Chicago's southwest side. Located in an attractive middle-class neighborhood with tree-lined streets wide enough for parking and driving, the frame and stucco house was about twenty years old with three 9 feet by 11 feet bedrooms, a living room, dining room, kitchen, and one bath. The house had an unfinished attic, a full basement, and a garage with an alley entrance along the south side of the house. This was by far the most spacious house and loveliest neighborhood the Tozers had ever enjoyed. But the quarters were soon cramped when Ada gave birth to one more son (Stanley) after they moved to Chicago. Consequently, the landlord allowed the church to remodel the house by turning both the front and back porches into sleeping porches. These renovations were started in 1931 after the last boy and child number six (Stanley) was born in September 1930.[13]

The Prospect house suited the Tozers quite nicely for a decade and a half, even after an unexpected seventh child, Rebecca, was born in 1939. Ada made do quite nicely, making space for everyone and arranging the dining room so that the entire family could be together for meals, and so that she could squeeze one or two more people around the table on Sunday afternoons. Ada took to heart Christ's call to reach out to the poor. Within months after arriving in Chicago she became famous for finding one or two of the poorest and loneliest souls from the church and bringing them home for Sunday dinner.[14]

If the Prospect house gave Ada room for her ministries of hospitality and compassion, it also provided the children opportunities for recreation. The backyard was large enough for Dad Tozer to play catch with the boys, yet they recalled he was quite awkward—"all thumbs"—and not particularly helpful in coaching them in athletics. Nevertheless, the boys enjoyed the yard and several of them fondly recalled nature walks with their father—complete with lectures on birds and trees in a nearby park.

If Aiden was better at nature walks and botany lectures than sports, he was best at shooting a rifle. Wendell said his father was an excellent rifleman. "He could split a snake crossing the road from many yards away." To keep his eye sharp, he set up a target range in the basement of the house at 10735 Prospect, and in the attic of their second home on Longwood Drive, where they moved in 1945. At both houses a .22 caliber rifle could be shot into a bale of hay with paper targets stuck on the side. Over the years he also took the children outdoors in rural areas to shoot. Even Rebecca, much to her delight, was taken to the country to shoot pistols and rifles, and she has charming photographs of herself as a teenager with Dad instructing her how to fire a handgun both outdoors and at an indoor commercial target range.[15]

The first Chicago parsonage was located about five miles from the church, and Aiden Tozer happily took two streetcars to the church each day. Harry Verploegh, a young man destined to become one of the three or four closest friends of Pastor Tozer, recalled that when Tozer first arrived in Chicago the Southside Tabernacle was a hastily converted and remodeled wooden building with a high ceiling, exposed beams, and two large boilers for steam heat located on either end of the elongated structure. Besides the open worship area, there were some classrooms and a tiny room for the pastor's study. Tozer never complained about the facility. He had served in less comfortable locations and he never coveted anything more. Nevertheless, within a couple of years after he arrived, the church undertook a building project on the adjacent vacant lot at 70th Street and Union.[16] Because the nation was in the throes of an economic depression, it would take several years to complete the construction project. But if this posed an inconvenience, it was no crippling hardship. Services were conducted without interruption in the old wooden structure.

＊　＊　＊　＊　＊　＊　＊　＊　＊

Renovation became the prevailing motif for the Tozers and the Chicago Alliance Church in the 1930s. While the building construction went forward slowly but steadily, Aiden Tozer also underwent a makeover, thanks to the constructive criticism and encouragement of several laymen, in particular Francis Chase and Harry Verploegh. It is to the credit of Tozer's humility and Chase's and Verploegh's courage that honest evaluations of the pastor's ministry were offered and accepted in a spirit of love. Genuinely eager to learn and improve, Tozer could laugh at himself and understand that some aspects of his wardrobe were, to put it charitably, eccentric. More to the point, he realized that singular dress could be downright distracting. In fact, Tozer wanted to be neatly and carefully attired. Years earlier he had learned the importance of "spit and polish" for his shoes and razor-sharp clothing creases in the United States Army. Consequently, through the encouraging counsel of Chase and Verploegh, the pastor began to dress more like a Chicago professional and less like a caricature of a bygone era.

Learning to dress in a fashion that attracted no attention became Tozer's goal and he accomplished it well. Indeed, the only things that were remarkable about his dress over the years were said about his daily office attire. Raymond McAfee, who served as Tozer's associate pastor for more than a decade and a half, reminisced in ways that have been corroborated by everyone who knew Tozer. The pastor would come to the church office from home early in the morning, "dressed in a suit and tie." Once in his little study "he took off his trousers and put on a pair of what he called his praying pants so that he would preserve the crease in his trousers for appearing later." McAfee remembered that these praying pants "were slit down the back seam some considerable distance." On one occasion "I said to him, 'how do you know how to put those on?' 'Oh,' he said, 'that's simple, McAfee, the back pockets go this way.'" The few men who saw Tozer in his study testified that he wore glasses and a green eyeshade. He was sensitive to light while reading and writing. McAfee remarked that "he looked like an editor in a local newspaper." And then there was "the inevitable sweater." Regardless of the season he seemed "married to his sweaters. He was always cold." McAfee, who had the wit and humor to match and delight his boss, "said to him one day, 'I figured out what you do. You take your sweater off the 31st of July and put it back on the 1st of August.' He said, 'You're right, you know what? I took a bath last night and what do you think I found? The sweater I forgot to put on.'"[17]

Tozer underwent more than a wardrobe change in those early years in Chicago. Although Chase and Verploegh were a few years younger than Tozer, he recognized their keen minds, wisdom beyond their years, plus their genuine affection for him and the church—both of which they hoped would bring as much glory to God as possible. Tozer's friends helped him recognize that some of his pulpit mannerisms could be as distracting as outdated clothing. While Tozer's sermons were extraordinarily well received, his tendency to pace rapidly the width of the platform, first to the left and then to the right of the pulpit, caused quite a few people to lose their concentration on the message. His finger thumping and the pulling of his fingers like he might be milking a cow were annoying to some people who were otherwise enthusiastic about their pastor.[18]

While Tozer absolutely refused to be poured into a mold simply to please the purveyors of polite society or popular culture, he thoughtfully and prayerfully took the observations of his young mentors to heart. The end product was a polished minister who could preach with anointed intensity that opened people's minds and hearts in ways seldom experienced in Chicago churches.

During the 1930s Tozer underwent an intellectual and spiritual transformation that proved to be as profound as the change in his wardrobe. Intellectually, Tozer had plenty of natural talent, but he lacked the advantages afforded to ministers who had the privileges of a university education and graduate study. In a man like Paul Rader, Tozer saw the effect of disciplining a naturally strong mind. Thanks to Tozer's own longings and intellectual curiosity, and the encouragement of an intellectual like Rader, he refused to slide into the anti-intellectualism that was all too common among fundamentalist and evangelical preachers in the early twentieth century. Tozer could say with all sincerity that "it may be a good thing I never went to seminary," and that was not sour grapes from an uneducated man determined to remain ignorant.[19] On the contrary, even after only a few years in ministry he saw too few Paul Raders and far too many men who were as boringly identical to one another as if they had been turned out of a theological assembly line after the fashion of Henry Ford's automobiles. Tozer was appalled at how many evangelists and pastors—even many with college and seminary educations—spoke with the same stained-glass voice, identically interpreted every portion of the Bible, and imitated some apparently prescribed way to think, write, and speak about God and His special revelation. Tozer and other thoughtful observers experienced the somnolence that came with hearing sermons with all-too-predictable styles, outlines, and deliveries with the "approved" number of niceties and decorative rather than illustrative or illuminative stories, all done in a manner that enabled astute listeners to discern within minutes the preacher's alma mater.

The Reverend Dr. Bernard King, who was well acquainted with A. W. Tozer and heard him speak on many occasions, remarked that Tozer's messages were always biblically and theologically sound, but presented with a freshness that was too rare in Christian circles. King said Tozer based his messages upon a wide range of sources when he preached. Particularly refreshing was the way Tozer drew upon early church fathers and Christian mystics. As a result, Tozer wrote and spoke with a "biting incisiveness" and originality that was seldom matched by anyone.[20]

Aiden Tozer was a complex man. He stood in contradistinction to the vast majority of his contemporaries in ministry. Many men who had the privilege of formal education merely saw it as a rite of passage to a career, and then stopped serious reading and critical thinking once they had acquired the coveted "sheepskin" and embarked upon full-time ministry. Many others who lacked the privilege of university-level education eschewed it altogether and chose to over-spiritualize the ministry. They often prided themselves in being men of "One Book" who were taught by no one but the Holy Spirit.

Tozer was not like that. He had read deeply of the journals, letters, and sermons of John Wesley. His mother-in-law had introduced him to the Wesley brothers' works, and he was profoundly stirred by John Wesley's declaration that he was a "man of One Book, but the student of many." The founder of Methodism exhorted ministers to read widely but sift it all through the lens of the Bible.

Similar to John Wesley, Tozer never remained satisfied with what he knew. He always had stacks of books to read, much more to learn, ideas with which to grapple, and thoughts to get on paper and include in sermons. In some ways, he was every bit as driven and ambitious as twentieth-century secular men who were pioneering real estate in the nation's growing cities. But what distinguished Tozer from his secular counterparts was that they wanted to earn money and Tozer wanted to know God and make Him known.

The commonly quoted phrase "all truth is God's truth" was no cliché to A. W. Tozer. He took Psalm 8 seriously and literally—leading him to assume that if we humans have been made stewards of all creation, then we must learn all we can about the earth and its fullness. Therefore he read books written for thoughtful people who were not formally trained in the natural and physical sciences. He became rather well-schooled in botany and enjoyed teaching his children various aspects of plant life.[21]

Tozer also manifested a keen interest in philosophy. He understood that one's worldview shaped most of how he understood and lived life, so he read some of the most commonly quoted primary works of Aristotle, Plato, Spinoza, Descartes, Hume, Hegel, and even Karl Marx. He also read surveys of ancient, medieval, and modern history. By no means a student of historical primary source material, he nevertheless had more than a passing grasp of what nations and their leaders assumed to be good and true, and worth fighting for, and with all this he learned at least the most obvious causes and effects of the rise and fall of nations and civilizations.

Although this self-educated man was determined to gain for himself the equivalent of a college-level liberal arts education, he certainly went beyond the survey course levels in English and American literature. He drank deeply of the American Romanticists, especially Emerson, Hawthorne, and Thoreau. He also loved seventeenth century English poets, among them George Herbert, John Milton, and John Dryden.

Tozer did not embrace all disciplines with the same enthusiasm he had for philosophy, history, and literature. He took a dim view of psychology—especially Jung and Freud—although it is not evident that he actually read much if any of their works. He likewise demonstrated disdain for sociology and anthropology, in part at least because he was a Christian humanist at core and took an inherently dim view of the social sciences. Actually, he looked with a jaundiced eye upon twentieth-century obsessions with "scientific methodologies" especially when it came to academic disciplines that claimed to "scientifically" measure human behavior.

Tozer was an intellectual, but he parted company with the modern intelligentsia over the limits of reason. Since the Enlightenment, the dominant thinkers have elevated man and his reason to the loftiest of pinnacles. The logical extreme of Enlightenment thinking declared that truth can only be perceived through reason. And concomitantly there are no limits to where man can go through the pursuit of reason—especially if the methodology is "scientific." Tozer granted that we can learn much from reason. But knowledge of God and the human spirit and the soul can be grasped only through the Holy Spirit. In short, some truth can be grasped rationally and naturally but much truth can only be discovered and understood supernaturally through God's Spirit and what He chooses to reveal. Tozer put a fine point on his theory of the validity of knowledge this way: "I am not anti-reason. I'm not against human reason. I am just telling you it's a mighty limited tool to work with. [God] is above human reason and He is above human science. The application of reason to matter, natural law, that's science and that's all science is."[22]

Ϙ   Ϙ   Ϙ   Ϙ   Ϙ   Ϙ   Ϙ   Ϙ   Ϙ

Tozer had been reading with fervor and purpose from his days in Indianapolis. The library and bookstores, as well as influential people like Paul Rader, pointed him toward the world of the mind. But his educational process was greatly accelerated in Chicago for several reasons. First, he had a bit more discretionary income from the Chicago salary; and second, the used bookshops were common and the prices often quite low. Indeed, two of Tozer's sons said that when they perused his library they noticed most of the books still had prices penciled in, and the range was mostly between ten and twenty-five cents.[23] Third, for the first time Tozer had some space at home to keep books, and his Chicago church office, although small, was grandiose compared to anything he had had before. Finally, the Chicago Alliance Church had agreed before Aiden accepted their call that he should primarily be a preaching and teaching pastor, and therefore he felt no guilt about spending numerous hours each week in his study.

There is no way to measure the hours he spent in a typical day or week reading books and wrestling with ideas, but it was substantial. In a similar vein, we know that he increasingly devoted many hours each week praying, meditating on Scripture, and seeking deeper intimacy with the Lord Jesus Christ. During the 1930s Tozer read voraciously, and he also developed a magnificent obsession to be in Christ's presence—just to worship Him and to be with Him.

The most succinct way to describe his philosophy of ministry as it evolved in the 1930s and early 1940s is this: Tozer concerned himself with the *depth* of his ministry and left the *breadth* of his ministry up to the Holy Spirit.

Ϙ   Ϙ   Ϙ   Ϙ   Ϙ   Ϙ   Ϙ   Ϙ   Ϙ

Aiden W. Tozer

Top left:
Aiden W. Tozer
Age 25, 1922

Bottom left:
Ada Cecelia and Aiden W.
Tozer at the time of their
marriage in 1918.

Bottom right:
The C&MA Church in
Stonewood, West Virginia,
home of Reverend A. W.
Tozer's first pastorate from
February 1919 to 1920.

The Tozer family in 1933. Back row: Ada and Aiden. Middle row, left to right: Aiden, Lowell, Wendell, Forrest, and Raleigh. Front row: Stanley in white. (Rebecca had not yet been born.)

Aiden W. Tozer, circa 1940

Top: Ada Cecelia Tozer, 1945

Bottom: Ada and Aiden W. Tozer, circa 1950

Top:
Aiden W. Tozer, 1956

Bottom:
The Christian and Missionary
Alliance Church in Chicago

Top: Aiden W. Tozer and Ada Cecelia Tozer, 1961

Bottom: The Tozer offspring in 1963. Left to right: Forrest, Lowell, Rebecca, Aiden Jr., Wendell, Stanley, and Raleigh.

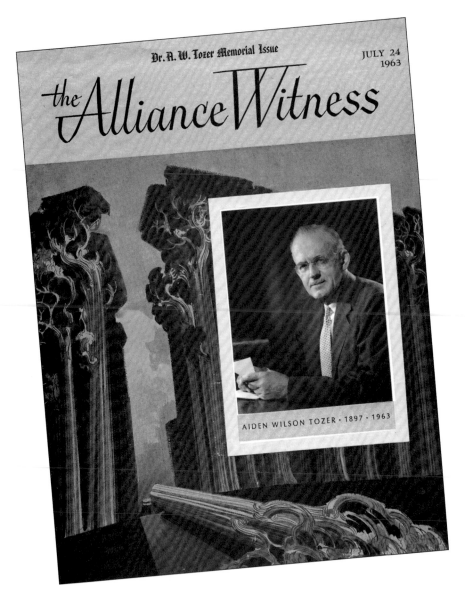

Dr. A. W. Tozer Memorial Issue

JULY 24
1963

the*Alliance Witness*

AIDEN WILSON TOZER · 1897 · 1963

By the time the Chicago Alliance opened the doors of its new building, the pastor had undergone as much of a transformation as the physical plant had experienced. His sermons were more powerful than ever, deeply penetrating the hearts as well as the minds of the listeners.

To the spiritually alert, Tozer had even more of the sacred anointing. His words and clothes were more polished, to be sure, but that was secondary. Like Elisha, Tozer had a mantle of the double portion placed upon him and this was evident in his preaching and teaching.

To the ultratraditionalists, Tozer was, at best, becoming an odd duck. And at worst, he was turning into some sort of "mystic" who could not be fully trusted. To other people who knew a lot about Jesus Christ but had never really come to "know" Him in the spirit of John 17:3, Tozer could be downright unrealistic. Such people found his absolute disdain for any methods designed merely to attract more people to be wrongheaded—even un-American. In any case, when he preached too prophetically in the tradition of Jeremiah or Amos, some people were offended and they worried that he would repel seekers and drive away many sensitive people.[24]

Tozer's style of ministry struck some people as unprofessional. He refused to network with influential people. He likewise voiced disdain for joining service clubs or organizations to make himself and the church known to a wider public. And finally, he refused to stand at the church door after the service to shake hands with the congregation as they left. Instead, after the closing prayer he slipped off to see the children in the nursery before they were gathered up by their parents. To Tozer, children were precious in the sight of Jesus and so they should be to him. Tozer, of course, had other motives for refusing to greet people after the service. He insisted that the tradition of "glad handing" people after the service was spiritually unhealthy. Such practice caused some people to flatter him for his sermon; and such behavior would, to his mind, harm them for their lack of sincerity and harm him too because he would probably begin to believe them. Finally, he argued that "diseased souls" invariably seek out the pastor and attempt to parasitically attach themselves to him.[25]

Whether or not Tozer's critics made any valid points about his antisocial behavior is finally beside the point. He did most things his way. He was willing to shed distracting mannerisms and archaic clothing, but he emphatically refused to preach less prophetically or spend more time doing public relations on behalf of church growth.

Tozer's obstinacy on these issues had the full support of his lay leaders, Francis Chase and Harry Verploegh. The church board to a man supported him, and the congregation, for the most part, was pleased with their pastor, except for the occasional voices that said their pastor should travel less and counsel people more.

*   *   *   *   *   *   *   *   *

A. W. Tozer's determination to focus on the depth of his ministry and leave the breadth up to the Holy Spirit actually bore much fruit. During the first twelve years of his tenure, the church raised thousands of depression dollars to construct a lovely new building. *The Alliance Weekly*, the denomination's official periodical, ran a feature on the new facility in early 1941. Complete with a photograph of the structure with its blended exterior design of art deco and Egyptian revival, the editor celebrated the church built "by Rev. A. W. Tozer and his congregation." The facility is thoroughly "modern in construction and attractive in appearance, both without and within. The exterior is of light gray brick and stone." The interior walls of this model building are "covered with lino, wall to windows. The floors of the auditorium, foyers, choir room, stairs and landings are made of linotile and asphalt tile." The writer noted that the main auditorium would comfortably hold 720 people, but another 80 people could be added without cramping. "There is also a balcony which will accommodate 124." To the editor's view the Chicago Alliance Church exhibited truly remarkable features. "The lighting is diffused from recessed lights in the ceiling. There is a circulating air system, which will provide equable warmth in winter and coolness in the warm summer months." This cutting-edge facility boasts a semicircular choir loft that seats eighty and a baptistery above and in the back of the loft. "An unusual feature," according to the writer, "is a Mother's Room looking upon the auditorium from the back of the church. This is soundproof between two thicknesses of glass. The service can thus be seen, and also heard through the public address system." Finally this fabulous building "has a full basement, giving room for the housing of a Sunday School of about 1,200, with all necessary equipment." And as an added bonus, "the old building has also been retained for Sunday School purposes."[26]

The new Chicago Alliance Church building did not rival the artistic elegance of some of the classically ornate Chicago churches constructed by the sacramentalist denominations, but among fundamentalist and evangelical traditions that existed in Chicago up to that time it was one of the largest functional structures with a careful eye toward Christian symbolism in design. No doubt artist Francis Chase and advertising designer Harry Verploegh—two men with keen eyes for beauty as well as function—had their hands in the final plans. At the front of the church, the overall impact of the design caused those who approached the building to gaze upward. The entire façade was framed by massive pillars integrated into the building's wings on either side. The pillars were marked by vertical grooves that pointed heavenward in the same way that six little vaulted windows on each side of the pillars drew one's eyes toward the sky. The entrance had two sets of heavy double doors, and above them was a series of small colored-glass windows, with a strong cross placed firmly at the center. To the point, the new C&MA church was, for conservative "low church" Christians, daringly rich in theologically informed symbolism.

Certainly this building revealed the mind of Pastor A. W. Tozer. A practical man who understood the need for a solidly functional structure to meet the needs of a growing church, Tozer already, in the 1930s and the early 1940s, was recognized as a man with his feet on the ground and the eyes of his heart increasingly toward the heavenlies, with the cross at the vital center of everything.

᛫   ᛫   ᛫   ᛫   ᛫   ᛫   ᛫   ᛫   ᛫

When Tozer became pastor of the Chicago church the adult congregation hovered around eighty people. By the time the new building opened—and estimates vary—there were approximately four hundred adults for the regular worship service on Sunday mornings. The critics who said Tozer was too prophetic to attract a sizeable congregation were wrong. As many as five or six hundred were attending regularly a decade after the new structure opened. Everyone agreed that the church appealed to people who were willing to be challenged to know Christ and follow Him in radical obedience, and therefore would never attract and keep worldlings who sought a social club and affirmation of their selfish lives.

Another clear confirmation that Chase and his coleaders had been providentially led to pursue Tozer for their pastor was evidenced in the impact he had on building a Sunday school program. Tozer firmly believed that all ages needed solid Bible instruction every week. Once the new building was opened the church attracted seven to eight hundred for Sunday school. Again estimates vary, but by World War II, close to thirty teachers taught classes of all ages during any given year. Tozer stressed the importance of Sunday school and taught a men's class each week himself. Furthermore, he helped equip such good laymen and women that his own class was comprised of only twenty-five or thirty men because such stellar teachers as Chase and Verploegh attracted plenty of students as well.

Always a teacher, Tozer loved the Bible and he felt compelled to help others dig in and understand the inspired ancient words. In the early 1940s he published a few of his thoughts about studying the Holy Bible. "To get to the truth I recommend a plain text Bible and diligent application of two knees to the floor. Beware of too many footnotes." He wrote that "the rabbis of Israel took to appending notes to the inspired text, with the result that a great body of doctrine grew up which finally crowded out the Scriptures themselves." He argued that it "is a dangerous and costly practice to consult men every time we reach" a passage that is difficult to understand. The commentators, he opined, "how disappointing they are!" By far "the best rule is: Go to God first about the meaning of any text."[27]

Tozer not only raised up a platoon of strong teachers, he challenged the church to press forward in spreading the gospel throughout the world. Like A. B. Simpson, the founder of the C&MA, Tozer kept the goal of sending and equipping missionaries continually before his congregation. During Tozer's tenure the Southside Alliance

Church was always among the top five or ten C&MA churches in missions giving, and at the most, only two or three other churches across the nation rivaled his church in annual subscriptions to *The Alliance Weekly*, the C&MA periodical that in the early and middle twentieth century was principally focused on foreign missions. Indeed, *The Alliance Weekly* and pastors like Tozer played a major role in helping the C&MA lead the nation in sending out the most foreign missionaries per capita of membership of any denomination.

Besides growing Sunday morning attendance, increased giving, a strong Bible-teaching Sunday school program, and core commitments to cross-cultural missions, still more evidence existed of God's blessing on the Chicago church and its leader. The leadership of the church was from its founding focused on building the Kingdom of God, not just planting and growing a local church. This foundational goal of Kingdom building was perhaps most apparent in the leaders' determination to call a pastor who could attract, encourage, and help equip the college men and women who attended the Chicago area schools.

Tozer became phenomenally attractive to students in the metropolitan area. Although local students belonged to and served churches of many traditions scattered throughout the municipal area where they attended on Sunday mornings, beginning in the late 1930s and early 1940s hundreds began coming to Sunday evening services in order to hear Tozer preach for an hour. Testimonies are legion from men and women who became part of the throng of "Sunday nighters" who swelled attendance to anywhere from seven to eight hundred. Tozer realized he was privileged to speak to so many college men and women. His goal was to encourage this younger generation to dig into the Word of God and partake of a deeper life with Christ through prayer that encompassed adoration and awe. Radical discipleship and greater abandonment to Christ would inevitably follow.

Beginning in the 1930s, students traveled from several local schools, but from two institutions in particular—Moody Bible Institute and Wheaton College. They came by buses and carloads.[28] Student numbers continued to grow as young people from Northwestern University and the University of Chicago also began coming. One woman came from the University of Chicago Medical School, and another brought girlfriends from Roseland, an industrial area.[29] Billy Graham wrote in 1952 that when he was a student at Wheaton College in the early 1940s, "I remember sitting under his ministry so many times in the Tabernacle in Chicago. I always came away blessed in soul. I believe him to be a man of God."[30] Gertrude Carlson, who heard Tozer on Sunday nights while she was a student at Moody Bible Institute, said she attended Tozer's church after graduation because she had been so blessed by the sermons she and a group of her student friends heard each Sunday night.[31]

What was it about Tozer's messages that enthralled young people enough to commute up to twenty-five miles in an era when there were no freeways and travel was difficult? Students would sit riveted to Tozer's messages for several reasons. First, he had a good sense of humor. David Enlow said, "He could make you cry and laugh in the same sermon." He recalled one humorous illustration even a half century after he first heard it: "He once said in sermon [where he was speaking on cooperation], 'Take for instance the [Chicago] Cubs— no, take a *major league* team instead.'" Enlow also said he was popular because he had "the supernatural ability to illumine the Word of God"[32] and this stirred the hearts and souls of these students.

One woman recalled that the youth as well as college-age people loved Tozer's messages. "He challenged us to be more committed and to avail ourselves of as much grace as possible. To that end, Tozer urged us to attend regular Sunday services, yes, but we should go to prayer meetings and youth meetings, and take advantage of the full-orbed life of the church." More than sixty years later she said, "I have never stopped."[33]

Missionary and pastor Dr. Louis King recalled that he met his wife while a student at Nyack College in New York. She had been profoundly blessed by Tozer's ministry in Chicago where she lived during her teens. Tozer had baptized her and she introduced Louis to Tozer while they were students. King said Tozer was not only an anointed preacher, but he took a genuine interest in students. Like many people who met the Chicago pastor during their high school and college years, King said Tozer led him to a deeper life with Christ, counseled him regarding ministry, and recommended numerous books for him to read.[34]

Men and women who heard Tozer while they were in college told me, "We loved to hear him preach." Others said, "He enthralled us because he spoke with a different voice." His messages were refreshing because he avoided the "churchy" voice and he loathed pompous-sounding God talk. He also eschewed fundamentalist and evangelical jargon. Instead, he loved words and used some they seldom or never heard—not to be impressive but for precision. An excellent communicator, he proclaimed biblical truth with simplicity and unforgettable illustrations. Tozer also endeared students to himself because of his transparency. He admitted that he was a flawed man and was not reluctant to mention his own shortcomings.[35]

Another thing the students found captivating was that Tozer preached on texts with references to his own experiences. Young people smell hypocrisy and they know the difference between preachers who merely exegete a text and those whose who have lived a text and have been transformed by Christ and the Bible. It became apparent to students that Tozer truly knew Jesus Christ rather than just knew what the Bible recorded about Him. Because Tozer had not been trained in Bible colleges or seminary, he read different books than most of the speakers students heard. They loved his enthusiasm for Jesus Christ as well as for books written by writers whom they did not know but who had a deep and personal knowledge of the Savior.[36]

If students were blessed by Tozer, they also stimulated him. He responded with his utmost for people who exhibited spiritual hunger, and such were those youthful souls who poured into the Chicago Alliance Church during Tozer's pastorate. When he saw their eager faces he was encouraged and inspired. They drew out of him the best he could muster.[37]

Tozer's fame, from the time he arrived at Chicago until the new building opened in spring 1941, had spread more than any other person in the Christian and Missionary Alliance. For better or worse he gradually became a household name in C&MA circles, if not yet in the wider world of evangelicals. Seldom an issue of *The Alliance Weekly* arrived between autumn 1930 and when the new building was unveiled May 31, 1941, that did not contain something by or about A. W. Tozer. He is mentioned or featured over 110 times from November 1, 1930 until May 31, 1941. Two citations were simply announcements of births of Ada's and Aiden's last two children: Stanley in fall 1930 and Rebecca in summer 1939. However, sixty-two articles—some short pieces and some longer published sermons—appeared over eleven years. Another fifty notices came out announcing where Tozer had spoken or was scheduled to preach, and many of these were engagements encompassing several days with multiple messages.

Thinking of how he found time to write so many articles and sermons—considering that he probably repeated some of them—is staggering. But when you add to this load the fact that he taught Sunday school when he was in town, and then preached every Sunday morning and Sunday evening for about forty-five minutes and one hour respectively, the work required was phenomenal.

To be sure, Tozer had few time wasters in his day-to-day activities. He did not have television or the Internet during these years, and except for occasionally listening to boxing matches on Friday night radio, or lying on the living room floor to listen to classical music from Chicago's fine arts radio stations, most of the discretionary time he had must have been devoted to his nearly consuming passion to read books, with the odd bit of leisure time set apart to visit used bookshops.

It is true that all seven children remembered periodic outdoor walks or the occasional times to shoot a rifle at attic or basement targets. But with the exception of Rebecca—the youngest—they all felt somewhat estranged from their father, albeit in differing degrees depending upon age. Lowell, the oldest, sardonically stated that his mother was a "single parent." The other boys did not use identical language but they all acknowledged that even though their father was kind and never abusive, they felt they never knew him. Not one son said he experienced intimacy with his father.

All of the boys except Rolland said Rebecca was Aiden's favorite child and that he doted on her and demonstrated more affection toward her than anyone else in the family. Rebecca confessed that she was, from her angle of vision, by far his favorite. She assumed her father favored her because she was the only girl and because she came so late in her parents' life. Aiden was forty-two years old when she was born and her mother was thirty-nine.[38]

The children all remembered their father's determined aloofness from relatives. He refused to travel to see siblings and seemed less than delighted if any of them showed up for a visit. Stanley remembered the thrill of visiting relatives on a trip alone with his mother, but for most of the children there was sadness in their father's purposive distance from both his and Ada's families.

Visiting relatives was not sacrificed so that the family could vacation somewhere else together. On the contrary, there were no family vacations. Once in the 1950s, when all the boys had moved out, Rebecca insisted that her father take her mother on a vacation because she had never had one. Rebecca recalled that inasmuch as the Tozers had no automobile she talked Ray McAfee, her father's beloved associate pastor and music director, to take them all to the Smokey Mountains in Tennessee. McAfee happily agreed, thinking it would be good for him and the Tozers. But, alas, Rebecca confessed, her idea failed to bring the hoped-for results. Her father was moody and negative, nearly ruining the trip for everyone. After a few days she confronted him in private, reprimanding him for such insensitive behavior. He acknowledged that he was dragging down everyone's spirits and made a serious effort to perk up. His mood improved but no one longed to take another vacation with Aiden W. Tozer.

Lowell Tozer remembers his father as being guarded about his childhood. When pressed with questions about his upbringing and family life, Aiden answered with off-handed quips or acerbic humor. It was impossible to get near him or his past.

They all saw more of their mother than their father, but even she kept everyone at a distance. As with their father, they knew she loved them but there was no way to be intimate or affectionate. According to Lowell, "We were known ironically as 'the Tozer kids.' But we were not a unit or tight-knit family. We were a family full of individuals."[39]

Most of the children remembered that Dad, if not traveling, was usually home for supper. This was the closest thing to "family time" that anyone remembered. On and off over the years, Aiden exercised his role as head of the family by encouraging times of family devotions. These never lasted more than a few weeks. As one son explained, the children just did not want it and they were seldom all together for extended periods in any case.

Whenever he was in town, Father Tozer did help do the dishes after supper. He also stayed at home all day once a week when there were little ones at home. He did this so that Ada could be at church on Wednesdays. This was the day for the women's missionary prayer meeting and she treasured this time. So Wednesdays became her day out. She not only went to church for several hours, she also went to the grocery store or other shops with Harry Verploegh's mother, who had become a good friend.

Aiden never complained about babysitting on Wednesday during the years when he was needed for the task. Actually, he encouraged Ada to go because he knew it was good for her to get out and besides, he had a high view of the efficacy of prayer and he knew the women spent several hours on Wednesdays in fervent prayer. They, too, knew the importance of prayer in God's economy, so they were busy at prayer and refused to be diverted by other activities. In fact, on some of the Wednesdays in later years, when there were no children at home to oversee, Pastor Tozer would slip into his good trousers, remove his sweater, and go down to greet the women's prayer group. He always thanked them for praying, and told them that he knew much of what he was able to accomplish in ministry was because of their prayers. They appreciated his encouragement because they knew he meant it.[40]

Despite Ada's day out during the 1930s and 1940s, she experienced much inner pain. Stanley recalled that many days as he was leaving to go to school, he saw tears in his mother's eyes. She never said why and he never asked. But he said, "I often went off to school with tears in my eyes because my mother had tears in hers. I never understood why until I was much older."

The other children never mentioned seeing tears, but several of them believed that she lacked a sense of humor. She seldom laughed and frequently she hurt the feelings of people outside the family with her blunt and abrasive comments. On one occasion a man from church drove some of the Tozer family home in his new black sedan. At one point during the five-mile journey, she proclaimed: "I don't like black cars. They show dirt too easily."

It is likely that bitterness at her husband's constant travels and his reclusion into his world of books had taken deep root into Ada's soul. One of the saddest insights into Ada's despair came from son number five, Rolland. He recalled that until about the age of ten, he wet his bed two or three times a week. When his father was away, his bed-wetting enraged his mother and she would beat him—even breaking a yardstick on him more than once. When Aiden was in town and Rolland misbehaved, she promised to tell his father and have him administer a good whipping. Rolland emphatically maintained that despite all his siblings' insistence that Rebecca was their father's favorite, he knew he was. "My father knew my mother's rages were extreme. Therefore, when he came home from the office, and I had been bad, she told him to take me to the basement and give me a good thrashing. He would then take me to the basement and close the door. Then he would say: 'Each time I hit the step with my hand, you let out a moan or cry.' After five or six swats he would then take me by the shoulders and say, 'Now you get upstairs and be good from now on. Don't let me down.'"[41]

As a youngster, Rolland (he changed his name to Raleigh as an adult) came to believe his mother's anger toward him was linked to the fact that she gained thirty-four pounds while pregnant with him. She was never able to lose this weight and she did not let Rolland forget it. He was too young to understand the role his father's career played in her anger, so he blamed himself until well into adulthood.

The extent to which Ada Tozer blamed Aiden for her problems is impossible to say. Most of her friends and acquaintances maintained that she never spoke derisively of her husband. Even the children were kept in the dark about her true feelings. To her credit, she never tried to turn the children against their father or even make them critical. Some things they read between the lines. But whatever they assumed, it came from inferences not her forthrightness. Forrest and Wendell remembered that she had an extremely difficult time feeding nine people on Aiden's salary. Both men said they were fed macaroni and cheese so often that they never wanted to taste it the rest of their lives. Although their mother did not complain about their meager resources, years later they learned from church board members that their father frequently expressed to the church his disdain for money. There were many years when he refused the raise offered by the board. Long after Aiden died Ada admitted to Robert A. Battles, who thought of writing a biography of Reverend Tozer, that he habitually returned half of his paycheck as a donation to the church.[42]

It is easy to imagine that Ada Tozer found her husband's excessive piety a bit hard to digest, especially since she had to do the grocery shopping and keep nine people in clothes. Aiden's refusal to accept salary increases actually caused many observers to look upon him as a most saintly man who manifested disdain for ungodly mammon, but those inside the family or close to Ada knew that his sanctimoniousness laid one more load on her heavily burdened back. To put the best light on this problematic issue, A. W. Tozer meant well but he failed to see the harsh consequences. To Ada's eyes, on the other hand, her husband's refusal to take a raise from the church was one more manifestation of his insensitivity toward her quite appropriate needs.

Little wonder, given Aiden's stubborn refusal to accept his churches' desires to help him care for his family, that Forrest Tozer took advantage of an accident to help his mother financially. Forrest had recently graduated from the University of Chicago Law School. One afternoon he was helping his mother with shopping when she tripped over a fuel oil hose that had been stretched across the sidewalk while a deliveryman filled the fuel tank in a local business. Ada had a horrid fall, breaking her arm at the elbow. Her lawyer son insisted that she should sign no releases with the oil company and he took over her case. His goal, he told me, was to get the company to pay his mother's medical expenses and also provide a modest sum for damages. But she urged Forrest to forget anything but medical expenses because "your father will not take anything from the company." Forrest recalled that he finally convinced her to leave it to him. He pursued the case and got her expenses plus a check for damages. With this money, he promptly opened a bank account for his mother and neither one let his father know she had her own little nest egg.[43]

By 1941 A. W. Tozer's ministry had enabled the Chicago Alliance Church to construct a new building, and his traveling, teaching, preaching, and writing all helped grow the local congregation and widen the Kingdom of God. Hundreds of people in Chicago and other cities were becoming Christians under his anointed ministry. Thousands more were becoming committed disciples of Jesus Christ, and scores of men and women were dedicating themselves to God for full-time service as pastors or missionaries. In all sincerity the Chicago C&MA pastor took no credit for these changed lives. Tozer gave all the credit to the Holy Spirit. In any case, Tozer—not because of personal ambition or design—experienced growing fame as a Christian leader within the Alliance and in increasingly widening circles.

A. W. Tozer was a perceptive man, so he knew the inherent dangers that lurked behind his spreading reputation. He recognized full well that God "resists the proud and pours his grace on the humble," and he understood that God will not share His glory with anyone. Consequently, he made a concerted effort to wear his popularity like a loose garment while remaining steadfastly faithful to his calling to spread the gospel through pulpit and pen. What he did not seem to recognize, however, was the irony of his family's brokenness in the wake of his successful efforts to build the church. He had no inkling that his zeal for God's house was undermining his own.

6

"A Growing Hunger after God Himself"

Ministry of the Deeper Life (1941–1958)

Pastor Aiden W. Tozer never complained about the multi-year construction project required to erect the new Alliance Church building on Union Avenue on Chicago's south side. On the other hand, he never disguised his glee when everything was finished and the church grounds were cleaned up. Building programs, he admitted, were inevitably distracting. Building materials and constant noise could divert eyes and ears from Kingdom pursuits, not to mention how the general messiness of paint, lumber, bricks, stone, and mortar created obstacle courses for pedestrians making their way to Sunday services.

Distractions notwithstanding, the church and pastor had not only survived the disruptions, they had done well. Membership in 1941 was up; nearly eight hundred souls regularly attended Sunday school, giving was strong, and there was a vibrant ministry to youth and college-age people. Southside's pastor had earned a well-deserved reputation as one of the best preachers in Chicago, and the national leadership of the Christian and Missionary

Alliance had recognized Aiden Tozer's giftedness by electing him to the C&MA Board of Managers in 1941.

Tozer's articles in *The Alliance Weekly*, like his sermons, gained attention because the author and preacher spoke with a fresh voice. He avoided the hackneyed phrases commonly employed by most preachers. And his spiritual vocabulary and engaging illustrations brought life to what many people admitted had heretofore seemed like dead orthodoxy. Tozer's messages—whether written or spoken —caused people to thirst for Living Water, hunger for the Bread of Life, and even desire to read books and enlarge their vocabularies. Tozer's ministry at once illumined minds and warmed hearts. In the final analysis, those who imbibed Tozer's fare were spiritually en- livened and hungry for more of Jesus.

Like the church, the Tozer home front manifested evidence of familial strength. Although not tension free, by most measuring sticks the Tozer family was functional and generally healthy. There were no obvious parental fights, everyone enjoyed good health, and all seven children from two-year-old Rebecca to twenty-year-old Lowell progressed intellectually, emotionally, and educationally at a level well beyond the national norm. All but little Rebecca were in public schools, performing well. And the two oldest boys were es- tablished in college or university—something only the most fortu- nate Americans were doing in an era when a high school diploma was considered a good education. Despite the fact that America was only recently emerging from the Great Depression, all of the Tozer children were urged to go to college. Indeed, the life of the mind, as well as the soul, was encouraged by both Aiden and Ada, despite their own limited formal education. The importance of books and education were recalled by Lowell Tozer sixty years later. He remem- bered that one of the privileges he enjoyed growing up in Chicago was having his bed in his father's home study. The attractions there were shelves of books that had been collected, read, recommended, and discussed by his father.[1]

The Tozer children might have eaten more macaroni and cheese than they wanted, and all of them had to find part-time jobs for their spending money, but they were blessed to be raised in an envi- ronment in which they were taught to read books, ask questions, and think critically. In short, Lowell said they were taught to love learning. The Tozer clan was also raised to respect all people, eschew materialism, submit to their parents and teachers, and in all things, to seek God's glory by obeying and worshiping Him.[2]

While pursuit of learning was a high priority in the Tozer family, and going to college lifted up as a worthy endeavor, there was a higher calling to do your best at whatever you undertook. The Tozers were taught that they could probably achieve whatever they set their minds to do as long as they worked hard. Aiden taught the children that becoming a professional person was not necessarily the mark of success. Rather, finding what you like and are good at, and doing it well constituted the mark of success. A. W. Tozer, Jr. remembered that during his boyhood in the Depression, he spoke derisively of a neighbor who had taken a job as a laborer with the W.P.A. (Works Progress Administration). Father Tozer heard the comment and then did what he always did when he wanted one of the boy's complete attention: "He would grab your chin with thumb and forefinger, and then give you a penetrating look that said, 'I want your undivided attention.' Then he proclaimed that 'a man who is doing a job and doing it well and not complaining is successful. Son, it is better to be the best garbage collector in Chicago than a disgruntled brain surgeon.' He then praised the dignity of work—especially hard work."[3]

* * * * * * * * *

By Thanksgiving 1941 there was much for which the Tozers were thankful. With the church and family both apparently strong, Aiden could enjoy some of the fruit of his own hard labor. The trips to New York City for the meetings of the C&MA Board of Governors gave the Chicagoan an accelerated general education in church politics and leadership styles. And walks in Manhattan opened Tozer's eyes to more bookstores, as well as to the numerous lifestyles of the Big Apple's polyglot populace.

Besides trips to New York in the early 1940s, Tozer was increasingly in demand as a speaker. He took on extended speaking engagements in such diverse places as Erie and Pittsburgh, Pennsylvania;

New York; Attleboro, Massachusetts; and Lake Okoboji, Iowa. All the while he published numerous sermons and articles in *The Alliance Weekly*.

By 1941 Tozer was devoting numerous hours to meditating upon and memorizing verse written by men and women who loved God and wrote songs and poems of praise to Him. The Chicago-based preacher became especially keen on medieval writers such as Bernard of Clairvaux, Peter Abelard, and late seventeenth-and early eighteenth-century writer Madame Guyon. He reveled in the poetic praises of eighteenth-century lights John Newton, Gerhard Tersteegen, Isaac Watts, and the Wesley brothers—John and Charles. Nineteenth-century lovers of God Frederick William Faber and Christina Rossetti captured his imagination, as did a dozen or more other writers whose lives spanned the centuries from 1000 A.D. to the late 1800s. These writers all helped Tozer learn to praise and worship God in deeper ways than he had ever done before.

Except for A. B. Simpson who died in 1919, Tozer found no twentieth-century poets of the deeper life to stir his soul like the saints of old. This paucity of twentieth-century pietistic poetry, in part at least, prompted this budding writer to make his own offering of mystical verse and it appeared in the October 11, 1941 issue of *The Alliance Weekly*.

Word of the Father
By Rev. A. W. Tozer, Chicago, Illinois

Word of the Father! Light of Light;
　Eternal praise is Thine alone;
Strong in Thy uncreated might,
　Sweet with a fragrance of Thine own.
The dark beginnings of creation
　Had their first rise and spring in Thee;
The universe Thy habitation,
　Which art and evermore shalt be.
Word of the Father!

Word of the Father! Truly God,
  And truly man by incarnation,
Born to endure the thorns, the rod,
  The shameful cross, for our salvation.
Our sins, our woes come all before us.
  We have no friend—no friend but Thee;
Oh, spread Thy sheltering mantle o'er us,
  And speak our mourning spirits free,
Word of the Father!

Word of the Father, hear our prayer,
  Send far the evil tempter from us,
And make our souls Thy tender care
  Lest sin and Satan overcome us.
O conquering Christ, deep hell despairing
  Shall bow and own Thy right to reign
When Thou, with joy beyond comparing,
  Shall bring Thy ransomed ones again.
Word of the Father!

This is the only poetry Tozer published. Unlike his other writing, his verse never caught on. How he accepted this lack of enthusiasm for his poetry is unknown, but given his habit of carefully guarding his feelings, it is doubtful that anyone learned the truth. In any case he was not destined to become a hymn writer or author of mystical verse like his heroes from history. Instead, he accepted the fact that he was wired to be a preacher and prophet, so to these ends he devoted his energy.

Issues of much greater gravity soon engulfed the Tozer family and American people. On December 7, 1941, seven months after the new Southside Alliance Church building was finished, Imperial Japan launched a massive air attack on the United States Naval base at Pearl Harbor, Hawaii. Thousands of Americans were killed and injured, and millions of dollars worth of military and private property was destroyed. The attack delivered a crippling blow to America's naval fleet, but it was not ultimately devastating. Japanese Admiral Yamamoto was correct when he responded to the information that the surprise attack on Pearl Harbor had been successful with: "I fear all we have done is to awaken a sleeping giant and fill him with a terrible resolve." Although the world had been engulfed in war since the late 1930s, American isolationists believed that the United States could and should remain neutral and stay far removed from the conflict. But this balloon of lofty idealism was punctured on December 7, and few Americans were untouched by the world war that would rage until August 1945.

The family of Aiden and Ada Tozer was no exception. They felt the burden of war throughout the prolonged conflict. The Tozers were true American patriots. They threw themselves into this war to defend America and liberate nations from German and Japanese occupation with a fervor equal to Aiden's determination to liberate souls from the clutches of Satan.

Aiden himself was a strong patriot. He admitted to his oldest son, Lowell, that he was disappointed he never experienced combat in World War I. Therefore it did not surprise Lowell that his father enthusiastically escorted him to register for the draft that had been reinstated before America entered the war in 1941.[4]

Forrest and Wendell remembered that from the outset of the war their father was emotionally caught up in the conflict. This was because the country he loved had been attacked, but even more because three of his sons served in the military. Lowell went into the Army, Forrest (Bud) joined the Marine Corps, and Aiden Jr. enlisted in the Navy. Rolland (Raleigh) lied about his age and joined the Marines late in the war, but the Marines uncovered his ruse and sent him packing after only eight weeks.[5]

World War II left few families unchanged. Compared to many families, the Tozers survived well, but even so, the war for them was traumatic. Lowell suffered first. He often said laughingly that lucky for him he was injured in Italy and then shipped to a tent hospital in North Africa, where he suffered the first of fourteen bouts of malaria. The Army must have thought him a lost cause, for they sent him to a Texas hospital and later discharged him. Forrest confessed that the severest wound he received in the war came from when he was hit with a wild pitch in a Marine Corps baseball game. Nevertheless, his commitment to the Marines and his country inspired him to stay in the reserves after the cessation of hostilities in 1945. He was called back to active duty when the Korean War began. In that conflict he received severe wounds in one leg that left him with physical disabilities from which he suffered for the rest of life, and from which he eventually died in 2001. Aiden Jr. saw action in the Pacific, but emerged from the war relatively unscathed.

Those who knew Tozer well saw how the war burdened him. Francis Chase noticed how "his face was drawn and ashen white." During the war, Chase recalled, "I would stop by often and we would pray together, especially when he learned that Lowell was somewhere in the Italian campaign."[6] The well-being of men besides his own sons concerned Tozer as well. Indeed, he made it a practice to rise early in the morning—several times at 4:30 a.m.—to take lads from the church to breakfast and then walk them to a streetcar as they headed off to war.[7]

The war brought more than burdens for the safety of friends and family of the Tozers as it did for many Americans. War brought social and familial disequilibrium even after victory had been secured. World War II scattered the Tozer boys to distant places and some of them never went home again. As one son analyzed it, "After the war we were never a family of nine again."[8] Consequently, the church helped the Tozers move to a different house at 9524 S. Longwood. This home was ideal for their postwar realities. It was a perfect size for the dwindling family, much closer to church, and located in a more upscale neighborhood within walking distance of two lovely and spacious parks.

*   *   *   *   *   *   *   *   *

In retrospect it is obvious that the Second World War and its impact on the Tozer family was more disconcerting for Ada than for Aiden. She, after all, had devoted so much of her energy and identity to family, and to watch it shrink—at least in proximity—had to be like major surgery, psychologically.

Ada's loneliness and sense of self-worth were exacerbated by the postwar explosion of her husband's popularity and the concomitant demands on his time. If Ada had felt unnoticed and taken for granted by her husband in previous years, this problem only grew worse after 1945.

* * * * * * * * *

Several factors helped account for Aiden's ever-growing popularity. First, he rose to the top of the C&MA leadership corps like cream in a container of rich milk. To be sure, he stepped on a few toes at the Board of Governors meetings with his bluntness and refusal to suffer time-wasting foolishness gladly. But to the minds of most of the men, Tozer was not only unusually intelligent, he had vision and he knew how to keep people focused on the main things. He earned respect because he talked little. Yet, when he did speak he had something important to say. Dr. Bernard King, who knew Tozer better than many C&MA leaders, said he urged others at meetings to stop wasting time on small issues and to remember "we are authorized, no, responsible for promulgating great evangelical principles and taking the gospel to the heart of enemy territory. Therefore we should never waste time on peripheral issues."[9]

Tozer's wisdom and ability to urge the board to stay on course led to his election as vice president of the C&MA in 1946, and to reelection in 1949. This new position meant that Tozer not only had to be in New York for the quarterly board meetings, he had additional leadership responsibilities.

Publications as well as leadership duties increasingly absorbed Tozer's time and spread his name. His writings continually appeared in *The Alliance Weekly*. In fact, his articles were so influential that many people said they subscribed because of Tozer's editorials and articles, and countless readers admitted that the first thing they looked for in each issue was something by A. W. Tozer. Beginning in January 1944 he contributed a regular column under the heading "Word in Season," and in 1950 he was elected editor of *The Alliance Weekly* (changed to *The Alliance Witness* in 1958). In this office he wrote a weekly editorial. And while these were not lengthy—usually

450–600 words—they were frequently quoted and most have been gathered over the years and reprinted in book form.

If C&MA leadership and a high profile in the Alliance's official publication vaulted Tozer to prominence within his own denomination, his books gained him recognition in wider Christian circles. He wrote his first book because the C&MA asked him to write one for the one hundredth anniversary of their founder's birth. *Wingspread: A. B. Simpson: A Study in Spiritual Attitude* was published in 1943. Although not widely read, this book did receive good reviews and it found an audience outside the Alliance among people committed to foreign missions, and those who embraced the Christian ministry of healing. Simpson himself, had been miraculously healed, and he therefore urged his followers to practice the ministry of healing prayer. During his lifetime he helped revive an interest in the Christian ministry of healing that successfully undercut Mary Baker Eddy and the Christian Science movement.

Four years after the Simpson biography was published Tozer's second book appeared, entitled *Let My People Go: The Life of Robert A. Jaffray* (1947). This little biography of fewer than 140 pages brought into clear focus the life of a C&MA missionary who pioneered mission work in French Indochina and Indonesia. Not as well written as the Simpson portrait (and certainly the subject was a minor figure compared to the founder of the C&MA), *Let My People Go* never found the audience of Tozer's first book. Nevertheless, this book placed Tozer firmly into the hearts and minds of men and women who employed biographies as recruitment tools for foreign missions. The inevitable, of course, ensued. Tozer became a highly prized speaker for missions conferences. Issues of *The Alliance Weekly* show that he spoke often in the late 1940s and throughout the next decade at missions gatherings across the land.

Leadership in the C&MA, articles and regular columns in the official organ of the denomination, and biographies of Simpson and Jaffray, all conspired to bring Tozer into the national and international C&MA spotlight. But nothing prior to 1948 did as much to make Tozer a household name in wider fundamentalist and evangelical circles as the publication of *The Pursuit of God.* Not one of Tozer's books—and he published nine before his death in 1963—

did more, with the possible exception of *The Knowledge of the Holy* (1961), to elevate Tozer to demi-iconic status.

The story behind this book is illuminating. It reveals much about Tozer as a spiritual man, it explains the source of his extraordinary anointing as a writer and speaker, and it helps us understand, in part, the lack of emotional intimacy in the marriage. A decade after Tozer's death, his friend Francis Chase typed a document labeled "Some personal recollections of my late good friend and brother, Dr. A. W. Tozer" for Robert Battles, who intended to write a biography of their mutual friend. Among the nuggets in this document written by a man who was at once brilliant, honest, and never given to hyperbole are these words he wrote on Tozer's own testimony about writing *The Pursuit of God*:

> He was invited to speak at McAllen, Texas, and he thought on the long ride down there that he would write on this book. He boarded the train—the old Pullman train—at LaSalle Street Station in Chicago—the days when you would pull the curtain on the roomette and he would be all alone. Well he asked for a little writing table which the porter brought him and he started to write. Along about nine o'clock the porter knocked on the side of the door and said, "Friend, this is the last call for dinner— would you want something to eat?" And he said, "Bring me some toast and some tea" which he did. [Tozer] kept on writing, all night long, this thing coming as fast to his heart as he could write, and when they pulled into the station, about 7:30 the next morning, at McAllen, Texas, that book was finished and all he had in front of him was just the Bible.[10]

The Pursuit of God immediately attracted attention. Beginning with publication in 1948 and continuing for well over a half century, this book has inspired and encouraged pastors and missionaries, as well as a wide range of devout men and women with hearts after God. Dr. Samuel M. Zwemer, author, evangelist, and leader in the Reformed Church of America, wrote an insightful introduction to the first edition. He confessed that that book's ten chapters "are heart searching and the prayers at the close of each are for closet, not pulpit. I felt the nearness of God while reading them." Zwemer described the book as "a masterly study of the inner life by a heart thirsting after God, eager to grasp at least the outskirts of His ways, the abyss of His love for sinners, and the height of His unapproachable majesty—and it was written by a busy pastor in Chicago!" Zwemer perceptively observed that this jewel of a book was written by a man "who seemed to burn the midnight oil in pursuit of God. His book is the result of long meditation and much prayer." Finally, the Reformed Church man got to the core of the book: "It is theology not of the head but of the heart." Tozer himself saw the book as a way to reach persons who have "a growing hunger after God himself."[11]

* * * * * * * * *

The Pursuit of God is one of the most striking manifestations of the truth that if a man will concern himself with the depth of his ministry, the Holy Spirit will take care of the breadth. Zwemer was correct about the book's origin. This powerful little book that has had such a profound impact on the souls of hungry Christians who crave a deeper knowledge of God was impregnated and nurtured in Tozer's soul. And the gestation happened in long hours of adoration and awe of God. Although the author never boasted about his devotional habits, those few who knew him well knew that the angular man with little formal schooling learned much about his Lord and his God in the secret place. Tozer spent incalculable hours in prayer. Most of his prolonged prayer time—with his Bible and hymnals as his only companions—took place in his church office on the back side of the second floor. He would carefully hang up his suit trousers and don his sweater and raggedy old "prayer pants" and sit for a while on his ancient office couch. After a time his spirit would drift into another realm. In time, he would abandon the couch, get on his knees, and eventually lie facedown on the floor, singing praises to the Lion of the Tribe of Judah.

No one presumed to interrupt these times of intimacy between A. W. Tozer and the Lover of his soul. But occasionally one of the men closest to him would climb the steps to his office and chance to see him on the couch or floor—totally oblivious to the world. Francis

Chase, Harry Verploegh, and Tozer's assistant pastor, Ray McAfee, all saw him at one time or another in one of these postures. And more than one of them mentioned that Tozer was weeping or moaning facedown in the old carpet.[12]

Spiritually alert Christians said that the "bouquet of the Holy Spirit" was all over A. W. Tozer. Others used different rhetoric, saying that he had the "sacred anointing" or that it was evident "he had been with Jesus." Tozer never denied that he spent many hours in prayer out of his increasingly demanding schedule. On the contrary, he maintained that anyone who wanted to know Christ better and love Him more must devote time to closet prayer.

Of course Tozer prayed at different times and in various ways—snatching whatever time he could to be with Lord. Clara Moore, a member of the Southside Church, said that after the Tozers moved to the Longwood Avenue house, Pastor Tozer would frequently walk the two miles to his office if weather permitted. She would see him walking along in his black trench coat and black felt hat at 6:00 or 6:30 in the morning. "He would walk with authority by swaying back and forth with his hands behind his back." He might well have been praying then, but in any case she knew "he would be going to the church for his prayer times that would usually last all morning." Clara was newly married to Merrill Moore, who served as an interim youth pastor alongside Pastor Tozer in the 1950s.[13] Unlike her husband, who admired Tozer and hung on his every word, she had no desire to emulate the pastor. Despite his genuine piety and his profoundly influential preaching, she saw things through a wife's eyes. Although Mrs. Moore did not elaborate, her comments revealed that she felt sorry for Ada Tozer. The woman was left to shift for herself and her busy husband refused to invest in a car. Clara Moore remembered "Mrs. Tozer coming to church freezing from the long cold walks in the winter." She saw her "trying to bum rides to get places." In brief, it seemed to this young woman that for Mrs. Tozer, life was "very hard for her."[14]

The conclusion is inescapable that the more time Tozer spent with God, and said yes to invitations to travel and speak, he drove a wider gulf between himself and Ada. She felt—at least to some degree—alone and abandoned, especially after the older boys left home for college and to build lives of their own.

Neither the seven children nor the men who knew Aiden well believed he was intentionally hurtful. On the contrary, everyone was convinced he loved his wife. But he hurt her deeply and apparently did it throughout their married life.[15]

Did she ever confront him about her feelings? Did she ever urge him to spend more time at home or buy her a car? We do not know. But one thing is certain. He believed he understood women and he was not reticent to offer quick and pat diagnoses for the occasional emotional outbursts he observed. For example, one day a young woman at the Southside Alliance Church was attempting to recruit older women as PALS (mentors) through Pioneer Girls Club as an evangelistic outreach to the neighborhood. When an older woman was asked to serve, she burst into tears saying she was simply too busy to take on anything more. Tozer observed the scene and when the distraught woman departed, he diagnosed the problem in a spirit of trying to help the young woman understand what had just transpired: "It's that time of life for her."[16] It would have been interesting to learn Ada Tozer's interpretation of the distressed woman's reaction.

· · · · · · · · ·

For numerous and perhaps tangled reasons, Aiden Tozer increasingly found time to invest in people other than his sons and wife. From 1945 until his death in 1963, Tozer poured seemingly unbounded energy into the younger generation. The Sunday evening services at the church on Union Avenue continued to attract hundreds of students as long as Tozer was there. They came twenty-five miles from Wheaton College, and they drove or took the streetcar from Moody Bible Institute. College-age men and women were eager to listen to an intelligent and articulate speaker who assumed the inerrancy of the Bible and used it to call them to radical obedience.

Tozer's popularity with students on Sunday nights led to other times of interaction with college-age people. Dr. V. Raymond Edman, President of Wheaton College beginning in 1941, became a close friend to A. W. Tozer. The two men shared many experiences and interests. Edman, born in 1900, was three years younger than Tozer. Bespectacled, balding more than Tozer and slightly heavier, Edman served in the United States Army as an enlisted man in World War I. Whereas Tozer was self-educated, Edman worked his way through university, earning a BA from Boston University in 1922. A Spanish major, Edman developed connections with Dr. Paul Rader when he served as head of the C&MA's Bible Training Institute in Nyack, New York. Through Rader, Edman connected with the Alliance and after marriage he and his wife went to Ecuador as missionaries. Eventually the Edmans returned to the United States because of Raymond 's health, and he went on to earn an MA (American History) and a PhD (International Relations) from Clark University in Massachusetts.

In 1937 Dr. Edman joined the faculty at Wheaton College to teach history. In 1941 he was appointed president of the college. Tozer's name was well known to Edman by the time he went to Wheaton, because as a member of the Alliance he had read many of Tozer's articles in *The Alliance Weekly*. The two men met personally by 1940 and became fast friends. Both men understood college-age women and men and sensed God's leading to encourage them in their faith. Tozer frequently had Dr. Edman come and preach at the Southside Church and he urged the college professor to write for the Alliance magazine. Once Edman became president of Wheaton College there was seldom a year that passed—at least until the Tozers moved to Canada in 1959—that the Southside pastor was not brought to Wheaton College to speak in chapel.[17]

Tozer shared his pulpit with Raymond Edman, and the latter opened the college podium to Tozer because they manifested almost identical understandings of the Bible. As Alliance men, both fully embraced the denomination's four pillars of Jesus Christ as Savior, Sanctifier, Healer, and Coming King. Beyond this connection, however, both men stood deeply committed to the belief that all born-again Christians are invited by God into a "deeper life" after conversion. Each man had experienced a personal and transformational work of grace after conversion. And while each man knew that the Spirit of Jesus Christ works uniquely with every soul, they nevertheless knew from Scripture, church history, and their personal experience that the Spirit of Jesus Christ desires to continue to grow in and flow through His chosen people in profound, transformational, and God-glorifying ways that are seldom realized by most Christians.

V. Raymond Edman laid out his views on what he saw as the liberating and fulfilling life in a volume titled *They Found the Secret* (1960). A collective spiritual biography of twenty people, Edman presented cameo portraits and deeper life experiences of notable Christians such as Amy Carmichael and Dwight L. Moody.

Tozer set forth a similar view, albeit not through historical biographies, but in a series of articles he published in the magazine *Christian Life* that were published in a little book titled *Keys to the Deeper Life* (1957).[18] Prior to this, Tozer had expressed his views on the 'deeper life' in several chapel addresses at Wheaton College—ten in 1952 and one two years later.[19]

Young people loved Tozer in the same way an earlier generation loved D. L. Moody. Like the world-famous nineteenth-century evangelist, Tozer knew how to communicate with young adults, and he had a sacred anointing from the Holy Spirit to reach people's hearts as well as minds. Like Moody and Edman, Tozer did not push Pentecostal doctrines or the gift of tongues. Instead, people were told that knowing about Jesus Christ, understanding correct doctrine, and being a good student of the Bible are only part of our calling. The Lord wants His people to "know Him" not just "about Him." In the spirit of John 17:3, eternal life is to *know* the Father and Jesus Christ whom He has sent. Tozer, like Moody, urged people to enter into a deeper life with Christ. Tozer often spoke these or similar words:

> Tens of thousands of believers who pride themselves in their understanding of Romans and Ephesians cannot conceal the sharp spiritual contradiction that exists between their hearts and the heart of Paul.
>
> That difference may be stated this way: Paul was seeker and a finder and a seeker still. They seek and find and seek no more.

After "accepting" Christ they tend to substitute logic for life and doctrine for experience.

For them the truth becomes a veil to hide the face of God; for Paul it was a door into His very Presence . . . Many today stand by Paul's doctrine who will not follow him in his passionate yearning for divine reality. Can these be said to be Pauline in any but the most nominal sense?

Tozer went on to explain this further by quoting *The Cloud of the Unknowing,* which he argued contained a prayer that expresses the core of deeper life teaching:

> God, unto whom all hearts be open . . . and unto whom no secret thing is hid, I beseech Thee so for to cleanse the intent of mine heart with the unspeakable gift of Thy grace, that I may perfectly love Thee and worthily praise Thee. Amen.

Tozer continued:

> Who that is truly born of the Spirit, unless he has been prejudiced by wrong teaching, can object to such a thorough cleansing of heart as will enable him perfectly to love God and worthily to praise Him? Yet this is exactly what we mean when we speak about the "deeper life" experience. Only we mean that it should be literally fulfilled within the heart, not merely accepted by the head.[20]

Words such as these set ablaze the hearts of thousands of young women and men who, admittedly, were longing for something more. Not that they sought emotional highs or spiritual "experiences." On the contrary, most of the young people at Wheaton College and Moody Bible Institute had encountered enough excesses in the burgeoning Pentecostal movement. This was not their goal. Rather, they wanted to know Jesus Christ better so that they could make Him known to a world of lost and confused souls.

Tozer's messages to Chicago-area students became famous. Soon he was invited to fundamentalist and evangelical campuses in other places. During the 1940s and 1950s, the Chicago Alliance pastor spoke at St. Paul Bible College (Minnesota) in 1941. He did Spiritual Emphasis Week services at Wheaton College twice in the 1950s, and also at Fort Wayne Bible College (Indiana) in 1948 and 1954, as well as the baccalaureate address at Houghton College (New York) in 1952. He also spoke at Taylor College (Indiana) in 1960 and Nyack College the same year. Wheaton College honored Tozer with an honorary doctorate (LLD) in 1950, and Houghton College bestowed the honorary LLD two years later. Although Tozer never sought to be called "doctor," he was certainly grateful to be so honored by highly respected Christian colleges like Houghton and Wheaton.[21]

There is no way to measure Tozer's impact on college people, but the testimonies are nearly legion. Billy Graham remembered going to hear Tozer at the Southside Church several times before he graduated from Wheaton College in 1943, and said he was always deeply blessed.[22] Dr. J. Julius Scott, Professor Emeritus, Wheaton Graduate School, remembered that as a freshman at Wheaton in the early 1950s, Tozer's challenges to "know God Himself," not just "about God," left an indelible mark on his soul.[23] In the same vein, the late Dr. Bernard King, who graduated from St. Paul Bible College in 1941, said he first met Tozer personally at the college commencement the year we entered World War II. He credited his relationship with Tozer that began at college as being extremely important in his spiritual life and ministry.[24]

Dr. Tozer had a range of influence on high school–age youth that rivaled his impact on college people. He frequently spoke at Youth for Christ rallies on foreign missions and radical commitment to Jesus Christ. Likewise he became one of the most popular speakers at Christian and Missionary Alliance Youth gatherings in places such as New York and Cincinnati, as well as Chicago.[25]

*　　*　　*　　*　　*　　*　　*　　*　　*

If Dr. A. W. Tozer had a special relationship with youth, college-age people, and Dr. Edman and Wheaton College in particular, an even stronger relationship developed with Moody Bible Institute. Tozer enjoyed a friendship with the Institute's presidents Will H.

Houghton and William Culbertson, who served while Tozer's ministry soared in metropolitan Chicago. Tozer became especially close to Dr. Culbertson, who wrote a powerful introduction to Tozer's *Divine Conquest* in 1950. And when Dr. Culbertson learned of Tozer's death he wrote:

> His ministry to me, both as between ourselves and in his public service, is a treasure which I shall remember. The Lord gave Dr. Tozer many gifts. As God's servant, he was faithful in the human side of the development of the talents God gave. Best of all, he knew the presence and power of the Spirit of God.[26]

Both of these Moody Bible Institute presidents were grateful for Tozer's profound influence on Moody students. And while there is no quantifiable data, people who attended the Southside Church during the Tozer era maintained that although many students attended the Sunday night services from Wheaton and a few other regional institutions, by far the majority came from Moody Bible Institute. One reason for this, of course, was that Moody students had a much shorter trip to 70th and Union than those scattered in the suburbs outside of Chicago. Student attendance aside, Tozer's influence to a wider audience than the C&MA was supercharged by MBI's invitation to do a regular radio broadcast with WMBI Radio.

Tozer's affiliation with Moody Radio station dates back to the early 1940s. Dr. Will Houghton, who served as MBI president from 1937 to 1947, had a vision to use Christian radio as a source of light to an ever-darkening world. Moody Bible Institute historians Robert G. Flood and Jerry B. Jenkins wrote that "as war exploded in Europe, Houghton put radio to work in the growing world crisis. The Moody Bible Institute, he felt, should be a leader." Consequently, Houghton "initiated a chain broadcast called 'Let's Go Back to the Bible,' that was aired across the nation." Flood and Jenkins reported that "in 1941 WMBI began broadcasting a full-day's schedule, and for the first time Moody enjoyed its own exclusive channel."[27]

A. W. Tozer fit well into WMBI's philosophy of ministry and communication. Never an entertainer, Tozer wanted to present

Bible truth to as many people as possible. Tozer's crystal-clear messages—all undergirded by his inerrantist view of the Holy Bible—meshed perfectly with Moody Bible Institute's mission.

Tozer was invited to do occasional messages during the 1940s, and the listening public asked for more. Therefore, by 1951 the busy preacher and writer agreed to do a regular Saturday morning broadcast titled *From the Pastor's Study*. Even more than the four books he published in the 1950s, MBI Radio's nationwide broadcasts made Tozer a familiar name among Bible-believing Christians. Indeed, Glen A. Lehman, the national secretary of the Independent Fundamental Churches of America, celebrated Tozer's influence on many of their men, and that his "own blessing included that of hearing his broadcast over WMBI."[28]

Although Dr. Tozer could usually be found teaching an adult class on Sundays, preaching a morning and evening service, and doing a brief message at the Wednesday-night prayer meetings, he still found time to write seven books while living in Chicago. The first three—*Wingspread* (1943), *Let My People Go* (1947), and *The Pursuit of God* (1948) were conceived and written as books. The next four volumes—*The Divine Conquest* (1950), *The Root of the Righteous* (1955), *Keys to the Deeper Life* (1957), and *Born after Midnight* (1959)—were less demanding, in that they were revisions of sermons or articles. Even so, Tozer was a perfectionist when it came to writing, so the work of revising pieces for publication took much time.

The only way Tozer found time to maintain a workload that would have killed men with weaker dispositions was that he and his church board finally agreed that they needed a full-time associate pastor and eventually a third person—usually a short-term assistant pastor or ministry intern to work with youth and help out in various ministerial capacities. In the early 1940s he hired his first two associates, but they quickly were called to their own churches.

Tozer's search for a full-time, and he hoped a long-term associate pastor, really began when he became incontrovertibly convinced that God's people needed to be led in theocentric worship. Over the years Tozer grew to love traditional church music and in particular Christ-centered hymns from centuries past. What Tozer wanted was a director of music who also had a heart to pastor the flock.

After much prayer, the board members and Pastor Tozer found their man in Raymond McAfee. An extremely handsome man of medium build and about five feet ten inches tall, McAfee had a heavy head of wavy dark brown hair, matching dark eyebrows, and long dimples that deepened when he flashed his winsome smile. McAfee was about twenty years Tozer's junior, but, like the older man, he was blessed with a longing for more intimacy with the Lord. Immediately the two men sensed they were spiritual brothers. Indeed, Tozer recognized in McAfee a man who would be a close friend in what they called his "Society of the Burning Heart."[29]

McAfee joined the Southside Alliance Church staff in 1943 and he remained a faithful associate pastor until 1959, with the exception of one year (1949) when he traveled to Africa, Asia, and Europe visiting missionaries. Tozer reaped enormous joy from his fellow minister, and McAfee always saw the senior pastor as his God-given spiritual mentor. The music minister served his boss in many ways.[30] First, he planned the music for Sunday services, directed the choir, and did much of the pastoral counseling. McAfee could put together music that fit perfectly with the theology of Tozer's messages. The senior pastor gave his associate freedom to choose all the music for a service. The only restriction on the music minister's freedom came on the closing hymn. Tozer always wanted to wait until the message had ended so that the selection could clearly fit the point of the preaching. Most of the time, right after the sermon, Tozer would ask McAfee what he thought should be sung. Neither man recalled a difference of opinion at this point of the service. On the contrary, Tozer sometimes prayed and sensed the Spirit's leading for a particular hymn. And then when Tozer would lean over to McAfee and say, "What do you think we should sing now?"—it would almost invariably be the number Dr. Tozer had in mind. To both men, such resonance became strong evidence that the Holy Spirit had led them to minister together and that His hand was upon their work.

Besides the application of his musical talent, Ray McAfee had still more to offer. Among other gifts, he was a first-rate preacher. Whenever Aiden Tozer turned the pulpit over to McAfee, the flock fed on rich spiritual food straight from the Holy Scriptures. Although preaching was not McAfee's first choice of what he liked to do on Sunday—he much preferred to lead the choir and congregational singing—he did feel God's pleasure when he performed ordinary pastoral duties. Whereas Tozer did not like to make hospital or shut-in calls, and because he was never comfortable doing home visitation, extroverted McAfee became a perfect complement to Tozer who was inherently shy in one-to-one pastoral encounters. And, next to the music ministry, McAfee reveled in classical pastoral care because he truly loved people and enjoyed talking to them one-to-one.

Because of Tozer's reticence regarding the traditional pastoral duties, some people were critical of him. In fact, one woman whose husband served as a youth ministry intern under Tozer for two years in the 1950s said that from her perspective the Southside Alliance Church was a "Preaching Center," not a real church.[31] Her opinion was shared by others but it certainly was not totally objective. To be sure, Dr. Tozer was a "teaching pastor." Nevertheless, McAfee and even the short-term interns saw to it that hospital patients and shut-ins were visited, and that home visitation took place, and all of this was done at Pastor Tozer's direction.

Raymond McAfee gave much to his friend and boss, as well as to the Southside Alliance family. But it was not a one-sided arrangement. McAfee earned a decent salary, but even more important, he had the privilege, as he expressed it, of driving Dr. Tozer around. McAfee recalled that "during the years I knew him, he never owned a car, so on many occasions, I drove him to appointments or to a restaurant for a meal." It was during the outings that the music director received a life-changing general education. "We would no sooner be in the car than he would be reading to me—Watts, Wesley, Eckhart, Fénelon, Faber, Guyon, Burns, Shakespeare, Keats, Byron, Wordsworth, Milton, Emerson, to name a few authors." Tozer not only read aloud, "he would read a few lines, put the book in his lap and comment for a while. Sometimes he would quiz me on the meaning of what he had just read."

Tozer taught McAfee to do more than read good literature. He urged him to memorize Scripture, pray over it, and then seek God's help "to enter into the truth revealed." Tozer's "method of teaching was the strong declaration of principles, never merely an involvement in word studies, clever outlines, or statistics." Tozer "saw the appeal of the Scriptures was directly to the will, and this was always his appeal." McAfee said that Dr. Tozer did not approve of teaching or preaching that elicited mere emotions. Sentimental and emotional appeals were not his style, "though I have often seen an audience moved profoundly by his declaration of the truth." Finally, Tozer "insisted that while feeling was an organ of men's knowledge, a man's will was the most important thing."[32]

A. W. Tozer also taught his young associate much about prayer. "Dr. Tozer was fond of observing that as a man prayed, so was he." Of all the lessons Raymond learned from his mentor, "it is his prayer life that has left the most indelible impression on me." Tozer allowed—even encouraged—McAfee to join him in some of his precious early-morning prayer times. And it was being with his discipler in this "inner sanctum" that moved the young man to depths of intimacy with Jesus Christ previously unknown. "Nothing produced such growth in me as those Tuesday, Thursday, and Saturday morning sessions we spent in this exercise." McAfee remembered that Tozer sometimes "would kneel with his face lifted, other times he would lie on the floor." While he prayed Tozer actually "saw the beauty and glory of the Trinity, and in kaleidoscopic splendor he would see this attribute and the other pass before his raptured sight." Like his preaching, Tozer's prayers were honest, frank, humorous, and intense. "His preaching was affected by his praying." Indeed, "preaching was a declaration of what he had learned in prayer."[33]

Tozer's investment in prayer time with God was, according to McAfee, the source of his anointing and power through pulpit and pen. What Raymond McAfee observed and partook of on Tuesdays, Thursdays, and Saturdays, Tozer did every day of the week with the exception of Sunday when the early prayer time could not be so open-ended.

The personally guarded and shy senior pastor opened himself up as much to young Raymond McAfee as to anyone with the possible exception of Francis Chase. A glimpse of Tozer's delight in McAfee's fellowship came in late 1949. McAfee had taken several months off to visit with missionaries around the world. Upon his return to Chicago he went to see Dr. Tozer. McAfee remembered the time this way: .

> When I came back . . . I went to see Dr. Tozer who was in bed
> with a cold. Now, he would never allow anybody to see him
> when he was in bed or when he was ill, but did allow me to come
> see him. I hadn't seen him for months, and I'll never forget when
> I walked into the bedroom and saw him, his first words to me,
> having returned from Africa and all these travels were, "Well,
> Marco Polo," a typical response. I went back to the church . . .
> and the last section of my time with him was greater than the
> first.[34]

Tozer enjoyed fellowship with McAfee, and he also recognized that this was a young man whom God had called to ministry. Consequently, in Pauline fashion, Tozer poured what he had received into this Timothy-like coworker, and offered gifts of time and candor that enabled McAfee to develop his own gifts to care for souls in ways that even his mentor could not. Tozer encouraged McAfee to understand that when a man comes to Christ he is called to full conversion. Offering his own conversion and pilgrimage as an illustration of what Jesus Christ wants to do in those He calls, he explained that in the wake of his initial conversion experience, "it not only opened his heart to the ministry of the Holy Spirit and the forgiveness of sins and the cleansing of the blood, but it opened his mind." McAfee recalled that Tozer said of himself "that as a young man . . . he was so ignorant it is a wonder the top of his head didn't cave in from sheer emptiness. But immediately," in the wake of his conversion, "his mind opened like a sunflower to the sun, and he became hungry, almost immeasurably hungry, and he began to read." He also hungered for more of the Holy Spirit, and his mother-in-law "laid hands on him that he might receive the gift of the Spirit." Much like the way V. Raymond Edman described people like Dwight L. Moody and Amy Carmichael in *They Found the Secret*,[35] Tozer prayed in the way Jesus taught in Luke 11—that is, he asked, sought, and knocked for more of the Holy Spirit. Some years earlier he also asked his mother-in-law to pray with him for a gift of discernment. And as McAfee observed firsthand, "indeed he had it."

McAfee acknowledged that his mentor "could be depressed and almost melancholy," and it is probable that some of this could be related to his keen sense of discernment about the church in general and certain people in particular. Seeing destructive trends in the church—especially drifts toward entertainment rather than worship, and following business principles and CEO models for leadership rather than biblical ones, and all the while being disparaged for speaking against such trends—certainly would tempt one to slip into despondency. In any case Tozer warned McAfee, "If you want to be happy, never ask for the gift of discernment."

Aiden Tozer indeed slipped into psychological despair from time to time but from McAfee's angle of vision, he did not remain there because he knew how to find a way out. A lesson Tozer taught McAfee was that when the soul is engulfed in darkness, get alone in the secret place and get into the presence of God. To the point: "A time of encouragement in the Lord's presence and he was looking down on the circumstances."

⁕   ⁕   ⁕   ⁕   ⁕   ⁕   ⁕   ⁕   ⁕

If no other younger man experienced the privilege of as much extended time with Tozer as McAfee had, many others saw him as a mentor for a season and have reflected on the privilege with gratitude. Merrill Moore served as a youth minister for two years, and his wife recalled that he was markedly influenced by his time under Pastor Tozer.[36] Ira Gerig served with Tozer for a year and a half from 1942 until mid-1943 and he, too, was encouraged and given constructive guidance. He pointed out that the Christian and Missionary Alliance saw Tozer's giftedness in teaching and encouraging young pastors. Therefore, they occasionally scheduled daylong sessions for the Chicago pastor to simply pass on some of his wisdom to the new generation of ministers.[37] Gerald Smith, who became a prominent leader in the Alliance including twenty-three years of service on the Board of Publications where he helped produce sixteen volumes of Tozer's articles in book form, recalled that Tozer was extremely obliging at these meetings for young pastors. He shared with them in practical ways. For example, he told them to be careful in their relationships with the opposite sex, and also to avoid getting caught up in seeking money. Particularly insightful was the urging with which he told them to avoid the pitfall of seeing the churches they pastor as "their churches," and to assiduously avoid references to "my church, my pulpit, and my pastorate." The men could hear him because he stood out among many other well-known preachers, teachers, and authors as being totally devoid of personal ambition and he never pushed his own books. At one conference he even refused to set up a book table and he said, "I am not a bookseller and I refuse to dignify my authorship."[38]

Another young minister who collected nuggets of wisdom from A. W. Tozer was Gordon Cathey. Among the treasures he gleaned was Tozer's recommendation of C. S. Lewis as an author well worth reading because "he is one of the few original thinkers of our time." Tozer also helped Cathey in his sermon preparations when he said, "I never go to the Bible for a sermon, I go to the Bible to see God. Then I get words for sermons."[39]

The Reverend Ed J. Maxey, who served as Tozer's assistant for two years in the mid-1950s, invested much of his time in youth work. Under Tozer's guidance he and his wife, Shirley, worked with youth and also did Bible study evangelistic outreaches in homes as well as in a south suburb of Chicago, South Holland. Tozer wanted the South Holland area penetrated with evangelism and a church plant. The Maxeys laid the groundwork for a C&MA church that was planted in early 1957. The Maxeys then went to New Guinea as missionaries, but Ed Maxey gratefully remembered his two years with Dr. Tozer. When asked what things he learned most from Tozer, he retorted that Tozer taught him "almost nothing about pastoral ministry." Maxey said that Ray McAfee on the other hand, "was an extension of Tozer's personality, and he did the bulk of the pastoral care." But if Tozer was "no example of how to do pastoral work," he did employ a man "who did exceptional pastoral work." Maxey did learn many positive lessons from Tozer. First, he learned to be more ecumenical in outlook. Tozer liked Mennonites and said they "love the Bible." He also had respect for the Christian mystics and encouraged Maxey to read in this area. Tozer liked Thomas Merton. And when one young man said, "If Merton is so good, why is he still a Roman Catholic[?] Tozer's response was, "You are such a good Christian, why are you still a Protestant[?]."[40]

Maxey acknowledged that he was not nearly as close to Tozer as Ray McAfee, yet the senior pastor frequently invited him to join him and McAfee for lunch on Mondays. After lunch Tozer led them to used bookshops and passed on his love for words printed and bound between two covers. The senior pastor got Maxey interested in the ancient history of Christianity. He also liked to buy books and he often bought a few and gave them to Maxey, McAfee, or others he believed would be blessed. He remembered that Tozer conveyed his enthusiasm for poetry to them, and he also regaled them with stories and history behind hymns that he loved.

Maxey admitted that Dr. Tozer did not spend much time on Sundays interacting with most of the adults in the congregation. Instead he slipped into the nursery and played with the children. The mothers who observed this loved him for it, and the children responded to him as if he were a grandfather. Indeed, the Maxeys' preschool daughter, Joy, became one of Tozer's favorites and the two of them formed a mutual admiration club.

This missionary to New Guinea, in retrospect, expressed gratitude to Tozer for what he taught him in those two years as an assistant, and the lesson that has stood out most over the years related to preaching. He recalled that a young man in seminary wrote and asked Tozer how he prepared his sermons. Typically, Tozer pointed to the Lord and wrote: "I get on my knees and manage to get three sermons a week together." According to Maxey, Tozer stressed experience before proclamation. "He said he would experience truth and then talk."[41]

All the while that A. W. Tozer poured himself into writing articles and books, preparing and delivering sermons, and mentoring young men, he also managed to make quite a few enemies. Discerning that the American church had become caught up in the post–World War II mania to make everything "large," Tozer's discerning spirit at first cautioned Christians to avoid the "bigger is better" mentality. And when he saw many churches becoming as gaudy and extravagant as the automobiles of the 1950s, with their loud colors and massive bumpers and tail fins, the Southside Alliance watchman became an even more outspoken prophet. Fearing that the church was becoming a cheap imitation of the world rather than a genuine biblical alternative, he lashed out against "personality boys." These pastors and leaders are, according to Tozer, taking their cues from Hollywood. They "shrug off impatiently the time-honored ways of the saints and go out for color, flash, size, vim, and zip. Quiet trust, stability, repose: These are passed up in a flurry of religious excitement." Tozer bemoaned the trend in which "numbers come first, so anything will do if it will bring a crowd." He went on to illustrate this development with this evidence: "The most dismal example to come to my notice of the shoddy means used to coax a crowd appeared on the church page of a big city daily recently." Tozer cited this headliner designed to advertise a missionary convention: "7:30 P.M. Moving Pictures of Cannibalism."[42]

Tozer's disdain for bringing business methods into Christianity can be seen in a letter he sent to Union Gospel Press in Cleveland, Ohio, decrying the cover of *Christian Life*, a magazine that billed itself as being the "Interpretative News and Business Magazine for Evangelical Christians." The cover for March 1956 featured a photograph of a new church building. Underneath the picture were these words: "This Church Can Be Built in Four Days." Inside the magazine was an article that advertised a manufacturer's prefabricated church buildings that ranged in price from "$15,000 to $35,000 and can indeed be erected in four days." Tozer said he wrote "in a kindly spirit but we must think of our young people!" This "shocking bad taste," he hoped, was not a new editorial trend, because if it is "it will be necessary for us to discontinue the use of [your] . . . material."[43]

If Tozer's criticisms of rampant cultural hucksterism offended plenty of people, so did his assault on what he considered "superficialities in religion." He appealed for a return to dignity in the church as he grieved over the decline of truly biblical and godly leadership.[44]

Tozer found disfavor among some of his own Alliance people

when he published the biographies of A. B. Simpson and Robert A. Jaffray. Always the realist, Tozer laid out a few of each man's flaws. Some folks, however, preferred doctored portraits. His brief biographies were "too real" for people who preferred plastic saints.[45]

A. W. Tozer offended some fundamentalists and evangelicals when he called people to a mystical—that is a "genuine personal relationship"—with Jesus Christ. He argued that any so-called personal relationship with Jesus Christ today must be mystical inasmuch as Jesus no longer walks the roads of this earth. But, because some people believed that mysticism sounded too much like paganism, they eschewed his rhetoric if not his point. On the other side, though, he aggravated still a different crowd, whom he labeled the "pseudomystics." To Tozer there was a well-meaning but misguided trend in the public prayer life of many Protestants. Tozer recognized that "prayers are not addressed to the listeners [rather to God], they are, nevertheless, meant to be heard by them, and should be made with that knowledge frankly in mind." The apostle Paul, he noted, "makes this perfectly clear in his first Corinthian Epistle." He continued, "We would do well in these days of superficialities in religion to rethink the whole matter of public prayer." We "lose nothing of spiritual content from being subjected to prayer thought and reverent criticism." His primary concern was over the "pseudomysticism which affects a tender intimacy with God but lacks that breathless awe which the true worshipper must always feel in the presence of the Holy God." Pulling evidence from history, Tozer wrote that "those who heard Luther's prayers have told us of the tremendous effect they often had on the listeners." Luther would begin in humility, "his spirit facedown in utter self-abnegation, and sometimes rise to boldness of petition that would startle the hearers." But alas, today there is too much "simpering spirit [that] sometimes expresses itself in religious baby-talk wholly unworthy of those who are addressing the Most High." Tozer found it irreverent "to hear a so-called Christian cooing in a voice indelicately familiar, addressing words of saccharine sweetness to one whom he or she calls 'Jesus dear.'" This is "a shocking experience for anyone who has once seen heaven opened and stood speechless before the Holy Presence. No one who has ever bowed before the Burning Bush can thereafter speak lightly of God, much less be guilty of levity in addressing Him."[46]

The anti-Tozer camp grew when on several occasions he celebrated the Scofield Bible which he said he appreciated and used, yet at the same time warned against some of its interpretative references. "What you need to do . . . is read the Bible. And you can read a Scofield Bible if you watch the notes." He said he had been accused of disliking the Scofield Bible, but he said, on the contrary "I've worn four of them out, and I have number five now at home . . . I just don't believe its notes. When it starts telling me things are otherwise than they are, I just write that off. But he does divide up things nicely for you." To Tozer's mind, to teach that the powerful working of the Spirit evidenced in Acts through the spiritual gifts presented in Romans 12 and 1 Corinthians 12 and 14 have ceased in later times because it is God's will, is an interpretation of Scripture based on experience rather than the plenary meaning of the texts.[47]

Tozer's critics emerged from other areas as well. When he wrote his assault on "The Menace of the Religious Movies," moviegoers found him to be narrowly separatist, and they frowned upon blanket condemnation of entertainment from Hollywood. Years later even he admitted to two of his children that he had gone overboard with his critique of religious films.[48]

Dr. Tozer stirred controversy with his occasional swipes at Roman Catholics. He insisted with many Protestants that the Catholics stressed works at the expense of doctrine of salvation by grace through faith, and he railed against what he understood as the Roman Catholic Church's use of "unscriptural impedimenta" such as "holy water [and] the elevated host."[49] Words such as these alienated Catholics, to be sure, but they also struck some solidly evangelical Christians as, at best, inappropriate misinterpretations of the meaning of Catholic practices.

Ironically, Tozer incurred heavy criticism from some Protestants for being too irenic and charitable toward Roman Catholics. From their perspective, Tozer erred by celebrating the writings of early church mothers and fathers such as Julian of Norwich, Augustine, Francis of Assisi, and Michael de Molinos, just to mention a few. These writers, according to some of his critics, were not ancestors of the church universal—they were Roman Catholics. Tozer handled these naysayers in the same way he dealt with negative comments from his frequent references to the Ante-Nicene Church Fathers or moderns such as Thomas Merton. These saints, from Tozer's angle of vision, knew the Lord intimately and he learned from their writings about drawing closer to Christ—even if he did not agree with everything they believed.

Tozer was a complex man who during his lifetime and even today defies easy labels. Although he was Protestant to the core, he learned much from the Western and Eastern sacramentalists. And to the surprised delight of his son, Aiden Jr., A. W. Senior demonstrated grateful charity toward a Roman Catholic chaplain who offered pastoral care to his son during combat in World War II.[50]

It was precisely this variety of nonsectarianism that endeared some people to Dr. Tozer but caused others to be critical. Tozer often received criticism for being too ecumenical. Men who knew Tozer well and were leaders in the Alliance such a Bernard King, Gerald Smith, and Harry Verploegh, celebrated Tozer's charitable and responsible "openness" to brothers and sisters outside the C&MA. While Tozer always counseled the C&MA to refuse to join the National Association of Evangelicals because he thought they lowered their doctrinal standards to the least common denominator in order to promote unity, he nevertheless grew increasingly nonsectarian over the years. If people or denominations embraced the inerrancy of Scripture and stood on the doctrinal distinctives of the faith once delivered, he advocated fellowship. Because of his openness to people of other traditions, there were always murmurings among a few disgruntled C&MA pastors and board members that Tozer was not a "solid C&MA man."[51]

Tozer was never an Alliance "company man" if that meant "my denomination right or wrong." Instead, he believed, for better or worse, that true love and loyalty was more genuinely manifested through fellowship and partnership enriched by constructive criticism. In the last analysis Tozer was indeed a loyal Alliance man. He loved his denomination too much not to speak prophetically if he saw even the slightest drift from true north on the biblical compass. In truth, he loved the relative freedom pastors enjoyed in the C&MA within boundaries of evangelical orthodoxy, and to his mind no denomination proved to be as obedient to the call to home and foreign missions as the C&MA. Tozer's own commitment to this dimension of the Great Commission can be seen in the way he continued to do the work of an evangelist even when he became a busy pastor, writer, and conference speaker. He also involved the Southside Church in local evangelism, and put local resources of time and money into several church plants in the Chicago metropolitan area. Also the focus of *The Alliance Weekly* (and later *The Alliance Witness*) under Tozer's editorship from 1950–1963, never strayed from its strong and purposive advocacy and support for church planting and foreign missions.

* * * * * * * *

The occasional attacks of melancholic or spiritual depression that Ray McAfee observed in Dr. Tozer were caused by many factors, among them the burden of his gift of discernment mentioned earlier, and also the constant harping from critics that all pastors receive. Of course, verbal and written assaults, like accolades, grew as Tozer became an increasingly public figure. These realities conspired to dampen Tozer's spirits from time to time, but his relationship with his wife also contributed to his spiritual and psychological pain.

Identifying causes of tensions within a marriage is difficult even when both husband and wife are forthcoming about the issues. And, in the case of Aiden and Ada Tozer, there is little evidence to conclude much that is definitive. Nevertheless, as revealed in earlier chapters, Aiden's choices in ministry, his work schedule, and his apparent lack of a good role model in his father, all conspired to hurt Ada from the earliest years of their marriage. It is clear, too, that during the couple's years in Chicago, changes within the family brought Ada both pain and fulfillment. During and immediately after World War II the five oldest boys left home for good, finished their education, and had families of their own. Stanley, the youngest boy, moved by 1949 or 1950. Rebecca, on the other hand, was not born until 1939, and she remained at home until she was eighteen years old, about eight years before her father died.

Rebecca, and all but one of her six brothers, believed she was by far her father's favorite child. On at least one level this is probably true, inasmuch as she was the only girl and her relatively late arrival made her a special gift from God in the eyes of her surprised parents. Rebecca had a good relationship with her mother, but there was a bond with her father that exacerbated parental tensions. The Tozers' only daughter admitted that she had a unique opportunity to be close to her father because five of her brothers were gone from home about as far back as she could remember. Stanley, she recalled, was there some of the time, but for the most part, she lived like an only child—except on Sundays when some of her brothers returned for a family meal. "Sunday dinner became family time. We frequently had a crowd. Some of my brothers and their wives and children came." Rebecca remembered that there were also the "stray folks my mom brought home."52

Rebecca loved those Sunday gatherings where "we had great discussions over a wide range of topics, including war, politics, or poetry. And no one put you down if you disagreed. There was always friendly but heated conversation." In her memory, it was all "very stimulating."

Rebecca had plenty of one-to-one time with her father. He encouraged her to read widely, and while there was no censorship, Aiden did question her and encourage a critical and discerning approach to books. From her father she learned to love books, and he devoted time to taking her on nature walks and teaching her to observe flora and fauna and develop skill at pistol and rifle target shooting.

According to Rebecca, Mom was not a reader—*Reader's Digest* was all she ever opened—and she never accompanied them on nature hikes or target-shooting outings. Whether Ada's lack of involvement was her choice or Aiden's is not clear. But Rebecca did recall that once she reached the age of eight or nine, she frequently accompanied her father to summer Bible conferences and camp meetings, trips she remembered with fondness because there were so many other children there. Indelibly marked on her memory, however, was that "Mother did not go." With no children at home to care for, "Mother could have gone to the conferences and camp meetings. [But] Father did not allow it." And no one ever said why. Rebecca did recall that one summer at a camp meeting her father took her for a hike. He stripped a piece of birch bark from a tree and then taught Rebecca how to write a letter on it in the way Indians used to communicate. "I sent Mom a letter on the birch bark and she resented this until the end of her life." Rebecca said there was something that drove a wedge between her parents that she never fully understood.

These tensions aside, Rebecca was not estranged from her mother who, she said, was a great storyteller. In fact, without her mother's willingness to tell stories about both sides of the family, she would have been out of touch with her family heritage because Aiden neither talked about family nor wanted any relationship with any relatives except his own children and grandchildren.

For Rebecca there were warm memories of growing up in the Tozer home. Mother's great stories about family, as well as Father's creation of stories about adventuresome rabbits, enriched childhood, as did the fun of house pets. There were always cats at home, and there was a memorable cocker spaniel named Buff.

The joys of stories and house pets, however, could not totally dissipate the clouds of despair that somehow seemed to be formed out of parental problems. Rebecca said that one source of her parents' estrangement centered on the fact that her mother was a romantic soul to the core, while her father, conversely, eschewed sentimentalism and displays of emotion, and seemed to fear intimacy. If this was not enough to cause a rift between the parents, Aiden's refusal to entertain or visit relatives—either his or Ada's—"hurt all of us," said Rebecca.

Because of these issues and numerous other reasons hidden in the past, Rebecca said, "Mother was a sad woman. She struggled to be cheerful," but sometimes the pain got her down. Both Aiden and Ada suffered from depression, and neither one seemed to know how to be truly healed.

* * * * * * * * *

Once Rebecca reached her teen years and became relatively self-sufficient, Ada Tozer found joy performing the ministry she had loved from the earliest years of their marriage. With nothing to tie her down, she moved with enthusiasm into her pastoral care ministry of visiting the sick and shut-ins. She also made pastoral calls—even if she never called them that—to women in the church who were lonely and needed encouragement. She also sought out poor or marginalized people, offering them encouragement and any other assistance she could muster. In addition, she spent time with women who were new Christians, pointing them toward ways to grow in their faith.[53]

Ada Tozer's ministry by the middle 1950s, provided a sense of freedom and usefulness, and gave her life new levels of joy. Nevertheless, there were wounds that no amount of service to others could fully cure. Some acquaintances of the Tozers who frequented summer camp meetings and Bible conferences said "she was never seen at these gatherings."[54] But they did not have the whole picture. After Rebecca stopped going with her father, Ada did attend at least a few meetings. Indeed, at one conference she announced to a friend that "I am Mrs. Tozer and nobody knows her." She laughed, but it might have been caustic humor.[55]

Several years after Aiden died, and after her marriage to Leonard Odam in 1964, Ada summarized her view of Aiden and their relationship: "My husband was so close to God, a man of such deep prayer, always on his knees, that he could not communicate with me or our family. No one knew what a lonely life I had, especially after the kids left home."[56]

How ironic and sad that Ada Tozer experienced such loneliness when Aiden was overheard commenting to a pastor not long before he died: "I've had a lonely life."[57]

"I Do Not Believe There Is Any Color Line in the Kingdom of God"

Toronto and Beyond
(1958–1963)

Throughout the 1950s, Dr. A. W. Tozer's reputation continued to spread. Seven of his books were in print by 1959, and under
his editorial hand *The Alliance Witness* had its largest circulation
ever. His radio ministry reached hundreds of thousands of listeners
each week, and his demanding far-flung speaking schedule to youth
and college meetings, sundry conferences and summer camp meetings, as well as national and regional gatherings for encouragement
of local pastors, all enhanced his popularity. Certainly a lesser soul
would have been infected with pride. But this man who had traveled such a long way from the mountains of Clearfield County,
Pennsylvania wore his widening fame like a loose garment. Never
impressed by numbers or the applause of fickle people, Tozer had
spent too many years reading the Bible and contemplating the
majesty of God to be impressed by his own reputation.

Nevertheless, some people—and even longtime members of the
Christian and Missionary Alliance denomination—saw Tozer as
caustic, aloof, and overly critical of churches that used gimmicky

methods to attract people that were trendy in the mid-twentieth-century church. To their minds A. W. Tozer was not a prophet, he was simply arrogant. But this was not a fair assessment of the man. To be sure, his style was sometimes abrasive, and his well-meaning directness could be hurtful to sensitive souls. Those who knew Tozer well, however, recognized that he had been called to be an Ezekiel to the twentieth-century church. Tozer's conviction that the church was becoming increasingly anthropocentric and obsessed with employing man-made methods to reach unconverted souls, rang true to the majority of the C&MA and wider evangelical rank and file. For the most part, Tozer's call for the church to repent and rely upon the Spirit of Christ was a welcome message.[1]

That this modern prophet was genuinely humble, even if his methods could be acerbic can be seen in his dedication to prayer. Tozer took Jesus Christ seriously when He said, "whoever abides in Me and I in him, he it is that bears much fruit, for apart from Me you can do nothing." To guard against a ministry with works that appear successful yet are fruitless, Tozer did only what he knew could keep him in a place to abide—that is, he spent increasing time in the Scriptures and in prayer. As the years passed Tozer increased his daily time in Bible reading and prayer—at once meditating on the Scriptures, praising the One who inspired them, seeking God's help in writing words with the power to transform souls, and applying truths to everyday life.

E. M. Bounds once said that a preacher who prays little is prideful because he thinks he can minister out of his own strength. Conversely, if an awareness of the need to pray is evidence of at least a modicum of humility, Tozer certainly manifested it.

❊　❊　❊　❊　❊　❊　❊　❊　❊

Dr. Tozer's devotion to prayer did not make him so heavenly minded that he could not see needs on earth. On the contrary, he exhibited a sensitivity to the poor that surpassed many of his ministerial colleagues. On the streets of Manhattan, for instance, Tozer and his fellow board members were frequently confronted by beggars. Some of the men were quick to brush the panhandlers away, arguing that they probably had more money than the folks they begged from. Tozer, on the hand, took a different view and always found money for a beggar's hand. Tozer was continually alert to folks who needed a few dollars or a word of encouragement. Furthermore, he was always encouraged to help the hurting by Ada, who had a well-earned reputation for caring for the most hurting and disadvantaged souls in each church where they served. Ada and Aiden both believed that "to whom much is given, much is required." And they knew full well that what they enjoyed spiritually and materially were unearned gifts from God. In this vein Pastor Tozer, who did not enjoy entertaining guests and the concomitant need for small talk that accompanied hospitality, never criticized Ada for her holy habit of bringing forlorn people to her table for Sunday meals.[2]

In the 1950s, long after radio and books had made him a household name among evangelicals, Dr. Tozer expressed joy in being among people from the lower and middle social classes. Other preachers could be upwardly mobile on the social scale, and view it as a sign of God's favor, but Tozer enjoyed going back to Mahaffey Camp almost every summer, and speaking several days to the economically disadvantaged rural folks in the mountains of Pennsylvania. He also enjoyed his regular congregation at the Southside Alliance Church. It is true he had some well-heeled members like Verploegh and Chase, but there were few, if any, high-income professionals in his church and, for the most part, his members were hardworking blue-collar people.[3]

During Tozer's years at the Southside Alliance Church, the area within a two-mile radius of 70th and Union began to change. Over the three decades that Tozer pastored in Chicago, foreign immigration declined to a trickle compared to the tidal wave of Europeans that flowed into the Windy City in the late nineteenth and the early twentieth centuries up to World War I. African-Americans, on the other hand, migrated from the rural south into industrial cities of the upper middle west by the hundreds of thousands each decade, as did rural and small-town whites who were equally drawn to the largest city in Illinois where they had dreams of earning more money.

The region surrounding Tozer's home church was just one of

many in Chicago that experienced population changes. During the post–World War II years, thousands of African-Americans moved into apartments and small single-family dwellings that were vacated by blue-collar whites who were prospering enough from the post-war economic boom so that they could move farther south and west into larger and more fashionable homes. The black population in Chicago by 1960 was well over 800,000.

These changes, profoundly affecting Chicago as a whole, also left their marks on the Southside Church family. Members and regular attenders gradually moved away to all-white communities. Some commuted back to their church on Sundays, but others moved their membership to churches nearer their new homes.

A few African-American families visited the church at 70th and Union, and some even continued to attend and made it their church home. But by the late 1950s, "white flight" had caused a decline in Sunday morning worship services.

Despite the changing demographics, the Sunday school held its own and even experienced a slight upward turn in attendance. The evening services, too, thanks to the college crowd's love for Dr. Tozer, continued to prosper in those years. But positive signs notwithstanding, there were increasing pressures to find property farther west to accommodate the Sunday morning people who grew weary of their long commute.

There were other pressures to find land and construct a new building. Some whites disliked being part of a population that was becoming increasingly black. They admittedly wanted to move the church to an all-white community. Tozer personally had no desire to move. That the neighborhood was increasingly settled by a lower economic class—both black and white—made no difference to him. Left to his own choice, he would have stayed at 70th and Union and ministered to whomever God sent.

Life in Chicago by the 1950s, however, was extremely complicated. While the one-time factory worker-turned-minister wanted to stay, he faced more than pressures from his predominantly white congregation. Many African-Americans who were settling in the Alliance Church area wanted the C&MA people to sell the church to them, and they made it clear that a multiracial church was not to their liking. By 1958 and 1959 several people wrote to Dr. Tozer when they heard the rumor that the congregation was pondering the sale of the building and relocation to an all-white neighborhood. One woman wrote to Tozer and expressed her sadness: "I oppose the proposed idea of relocating the church: (1) selfishly I benefit" from the church being where it is now and I "would not likely be able to travel further . . . south or west." Also, she said, as a student (2) "there are other students who feel the same way." Finally, she sensed "a sickening kind of irony for a church that so emphasizes the missionary aspect to vacate a mission field that is literally coming to it."[4]

Dr. Tozer promptly responded. He expressed gratitude to learn that the church had encouraged her. Then he confessed that "the matter of moving is one that bothers me very much." He went on to say that from his point of view and the perspective of 90 percent of the members, "it would be perfectly all right to have half our church members be colored. It would not bother me in the slightest. In fact, I think I should enjoy it."

Tozer continued:

> However, the facts are these: The colored march on the South Side is a determined thing. The colored people do not want to integrate with the whites. They want the whites to get out, and they are saying so in no uncertain terms. The failure to integrate is not the result of reservation on the part of our people but on the part of the colored people themselves. They have had at least one parade declaring their intention to take over Englewood and Brainerd, and have passed around dodgers in the apartment houses around our church demanding that white people get out and let the colored people come in.
>
> This puts quite another face on the whole matter, as you will undoubtedly agree. Please continue to pray.[5]

Two months later Pastor Tozer received mail from another woman—a "newcomer to Chicago"—who implored him not to move the church because there are so few Bible-teaching churches on the South Side.[6]

More letters arrived on the same subject. One came from Saginaw,

Michigan. A pastor there had heard about the Southside church's problem of "integration or relocation" and he offered advice on finding ways to integrate, because "whichever way it goes it will affect the evangelical witness to the Negroes throughout the country."[7]

Tozer fully understood the testimony that comes from such decisions about moving and staying. But he also knew that although there were African-Americans on the South Side who wanted an integrated church, others counseled that the C&MA witness would be more positive in the eyes of the blacks if the whites would sell the building to them. To the point, while some blacks and whites genuinely wanted to integrate, people from both ethnic groups stood in determined opposition.

Despite the fact that blacks began moving to Chicago in large numbers during World War I, the city never practiced segregation in most public accommodations. Nevertheless, racial tensions were often strong because many whites, especially among the poorly educated working classes, disliked blacks moving into their local communities and places of work. In 1919, for example, a race riot broke out that lasted five days and only ended after twenty-three blacks and fifteen whites were killed and the Illinois National Guard restored order.[8]

African-Americans continued to emigrate to Chicago after the riots, but housing was never easy for them to find. Gradually, however, these rural black people—slowly and agonizingly in the face of white opposition—found places to rent or purchase in a steadily widening area on the Windy City's south side. While some blacks were grateful to integrate the residential neighborhoods, others quite purposefully made it known that they wanted the whites to move. While some of these black "segregationists" were simply as bigoted as many whites, there was a rather practical issue involved. Whites could move almost anywhere and not face a color line. If they had the money, they could resettle in most communities. Blacks, on the other hand, were sorely limited in their geographic mobility even if they had the money. Banks frequently "redlined" neighborhoods by simply refusing to make home loans to blacks. And after World War II, Chicago had a reputation for being hostile to blacks who attempted to move into all-white neighborhoods. In

Chicago's Cicero area, for example, a black family that had purchased a house and moved in was forcibly driven out in 1951 by a white mob that damaged the exterior of the house, smashed out the windows, and verbally attacked the helpless family.[9]

The Cicero incident was not isolated, and furthermore, blacks who wanted to have their own church buildings for their own denominations, faced the nonracial issue of the economics of taxes. The city, county, and various townships did not want to take property off of the tax rolls for new churches. Therefore, black denominational leaders had little recourse other than purchasing churches already off the tax rolls—and these were mostly owned by whites.

These tangled realities explain, in part at least, why some blacks pressed A. W. Tozer's church to move on and sell to them. The issue of tax-exempt property for churches, in fact emerged as a point where the idealism of some blacks and whites, who wanted integration, crashed into the harsh realities of tax-hungry local governments.

Finally, Tozer realized the leadership had made up its collective mind. The building must be sold, property acquired away from the South Side, and a new facility built. Although Pastor Tozer acknowledged the church's authority to make this choice, he also knew his own limitations. He agreed to support the decision but told everyone that he had neither the energy nor sense of calling from God to oversee a move and a building program. Francis Chase recalled that Tozer became deeply grieved over the gradual disintegration of the unity that they had once enjoyed in the neighborhood and church, and he accepted the decision to move. But he told the church that "now, at this stage of my life I don't think that I could possibly go through another building campaign, nor to continue long as your pastor for I can't possibly do what I know God wants me to do . . . and be the pastor of this church, and especially go through this building program."[10]

In the midst of these trials of the late 1950s, Tozer never lost his productivity or his sense of humor. He published *Born after Midnight* in 1959 and had managed to get all the writing done for a volume titled *Of God and Men* that came out in 1960. His speaking schedule in and outside the church remained heavy as well. Because he had received two honorary doctorates in recent years, and inasmuch as his publication list was growing and attracting increased attention, everyone "around the church," according to Francis Chase, "started to call him 'Doctor,' but he remained one of us" with his usual sense of humor. One day when someone addressed him as doctor, he replied, "I'm still an intern."[11]

When word spread that Chicago's celebrated pastor had resigned, scores of churches attempted to attract him. But Tozer had a keen sense that God was calling him to concentrate on writing and speaking without any responsibilities to oversee a local church. Therefore, he turned away every feeler and offer.

When people concluded Tozer must be retiring, he corrected them. "I will preach as long as I can hold a Bible." He jocularly acknowledged that the Levites might have finished their ministry at age fifty, "but prophets never retired, so I'm not retiring, except to put on new tires to go a little faster and farther."[12]

Tozer made it known publicly that he intended to devote his energies to writing and conference speaking and to continue his work as editor of *The Alliance Witness*. To that end, he suggested his desire to relocate in the New York area, so as to be close to the offices of the Christian and Missionary Alliance.[13]

The second-largest Protestant church in Toronto, Ontario—Avenue Road Church in the heart of the city—had recently aligned with the C&MA. This church wanted Tozer because their goal was to reach the students at the University of Toronto. For several years Avenue Road Church worked closely with the University's InterVarsity Christian Fellowship chapter, and they all knew Tozer could reach these students. The church contacted Tozer and asked him to consider their open pastorate. He immediately refused, thanking them, but insisting that he was no longer called to pastor a church.[14]

The Avenue Road leaders contacted District Superintendent William J. Newell, asking, "What will it take to get Dr. Tozer here as our pastor?" He responded, "I believe I know how to get your candidate here. Pray for me; I am going to give him a telephone call." Newell called Tozer and asked him if he would at least preach one Sunday morning and evening at Avenue Road Alliance Church. He responded, "I'll go anywhere to preach, but it needs to be clear that I am not interested in being pastor of Avenue Road Church."[15]

Tozer went to Toronto and spoke at the morning and evening services. He was well received and the congregation—including many university students—was eager to have him again. Consequently the church board, in consultation with William Newell, made Tozer an offer he neither anticipated nor was able to refuse. They acknowledged Tozer's refusal to serve as a local church pastor. The men told Tozer they had a young man who agreed to become their pastor, "but would you be willing simply to preach here twice each Sunday?" The young man who will be our pastor "will handle everything. You won't have to attend board meetings, visit the sick, lay any cornerstones, attend any picnics, cut any ribbons or anything else. Just preach twice a Sunday, that's all." A. W. Tozer was speechless. Here he had an offer to become the preaching minister responsible for only two sermons on Sunday and the rest of his time free to conduct Alliance business, travel, and speak. He agreed to pray and respond within a week.[16]

How much he considered Ada's desires is unknown. But within a few days he telephoned Toronto and accepted the call. By December 1959 he and Ada alone—even Rebecca was now out on her own—embarked upon the most fruitful season of both their lives.

*　*　*　*　*　*　*　*　*

The largest evangelical church in Toronto was pastored by Oswald J. Smith, a famous and magnetic preacher and author of numerous devotional books. There were few evangelical churches in Ontario's largest city, so Smith's church was regularly packed with people hungry to hear Bible-based, prophetic preaching. Within a year, however, Avenue Road Church had become the largest church in Toronto. This was not because Tozer set out on a campaign to be number one. On the contrary, he admired Oswald Smith and his preaching and felt no desire to compete. But Smith was frequently absent from his pulpit, being one of the most sought-after evangelical preachers in North America. Consequently, people drifted over to

Avenue Road because Tozer was keeping his promise to be in the pulpit twice on Sundays—except for rare exceptions.

Furthermore, there was the matter of university students. Probably no preacher in the United States and Canada captured the minds and hearts of college-age people like A. W. Tozer. Therefore, within a year and a half, Avenue Road Church was filled to capacity at both services, and at least a third of the congregants at the standing-room-only services were college and university people whom Tozer loved to encourage.[17]

❦ ❦ ❦ ❦ ❦ ❦ ❦ ❦ ❦ ❦

For the next three and a half years from early 1960 until spring 1963, Aiden W. Tozer hit his stride as a preacher and writer. His book *Of God and Men*, which he said simply focused on "God and men and their relation to each other—this I believe to be all that really matters in this world, and this is what I have written about here," came off the presses in 1960.[18] The following year a book that many people think is Tozer's magnum opus, *The Knowledge of the Holy*, made its debut with Harper Publishers. This was his only book among nine published in his lifetime to be done with a major secular press. All his other books were produced by Christian Publications, the official publisher of the C&MA.

Several factors conspired to make *The Knowledge of the Holy* Tozer's bestselling book— then and now. First, Harper's was a mainline and well-established publishing house. The Harper imprint was prestigious because they published numerous first-rate authors, whom they promoted through distributors who had access to wide markets. Second, Tozer had become internationally acclaimed. Dr. Martyn Lloyd-Jones, for example, the celebrated preacher who held one of the most influential pulpits in the English-speaking world, had been urging Tozer to come and preach at his church in London. Also, by 1960 many of Tozer's *Alliance* articles were regularly reprinted in *Life of Faith*, a British periodical widely read by evangelicals in the United Kingdom. But equally important in accounting for wide sales was the subject matter of the book and the way this seasoned author developed it.

The Pursuit of God, if never as popular as *The Knowledge of the Holy*, proved to be a popular book—one through which the obviously anointed author eagerly fed, as he phrased it, those "increasing numbers of persons whose religious lives are marked by a growing hunger after God Himself," people "eager for spiritual realities . . . a thirst for God . . ." Tozer prayed that this book would encourage revival for which his heart and soul longed; and he believed that the thirst abroad for Living Water to be "the only harbinger of revival which I have been able to detect anywhere on the religious horizon."[19]

These words were penned soon after in World War II. But by 1961, nearly twenty years later, when he wrote *The Knowledge of the Holy*, the religious scene had changed. Tozer no longer saw signs of revival. On the contrary, having spent eighteen more years in prayer since the publication of *The Pursuit of God*, and having crisscrossed the United States and Canada preaching and urging people to join him in the "Society of the Burning Heart," he had come to see, alas, that most people (including Christians) had such a low view of God that they felt little desire to pursue Him. Religious hucksters, as well as other purveyors of cheap grace, from Tozer's angle of vision, had horridly diminished people's image of God. As Tozer imbibed the Christian mystics who marveled at the majesty and splendor of The Holy God—The Glorious One who poured out His "Amazing Grace" on us sinners, and as he drank deeply at the well of the deeper life, he became convinced that "the Church has surrendered her once lofty concept of God and has substituted for it one so low, so ignoble, as to be utterly unworthy of thinking, worshipping men."

Tozer reasoned that the church had not done this deliberately, "but little by little and without her knowledge; and her very unawareness only makes her situation all the more tragic." Tozer saw "a hundred lesser evils everywhere among us" because of this "low view of God." After we lost our "sense of the majesty has come the further loss of religious awe and consciousness of the divine Presence." To put a fine point on it, "we have lost our spirit of worship and our ability to withdraw inwardly to meet God in adoring silence." Christianity by the early 1960s "is simply not producing the kind of Christian who can appreciate or experience the Life of the Spirit." This is why Tozer wrote *The Knowledge of the Holy*, in which he presented over twenty attributes of God with commentary on "their meaning in the Christian life."[20]

This splendid volume struck a chord in the hearts of Christians—many of whom were similar to the Samaritan woman at the well. Jesus told her, and Tozer's new book helped others two thousand years later to hear Him again: "You worship what you do not know."

The Knowledge of the Holy: The Attributes of God: Their Meaning in the Christian Life, was a succinct statement from a man who wanted people to join him in seeing the character and attributes of God as He has chosen to reveal them, and through this vision, to fall down with him before the throne, with exultant words of praise.

Tozer understood people because he listened, and he also vividly recalled his own past. He realized that when people are just beginning to open their eyes to the majesty of God, they simply do not know how to praise Him. Therefore, he set out to prepare another book that he envisioned as a sequel to *The Knowledge of the Holy* titled *The Christian Book of Mystical Verse*. The powerful preacher designed this little book as an aid to worship. He selected more than a hundred of his favorite "mystical verses," and arranged them in categories to help people learn to worship the Living God. He explained that "mystical," although long an unacceptable word among evangelicals, actually applies to such lights as Charles Wesley, Isaac Watts, John Newton, and a host of other names—including the apostle Paul, Moses, and King David. These "mystics" are not "emotionally unstable, visionary, and worst of all, unsound theologically." Rather, "I refer to the evangelical mystic who has "been brought by the gospel into intimate fellowship with the Godhead. His theology is no less and no more than is taught in the Christian Scriptures." Like the saints of old, including "martyrs, reformers, Puritans, evangelists, and missionaries of the cross," each one differs "from the ordinary Orthodox Christian only because he experiences his faith down in the depths of his sentient being while the other does not." In short, the mystic "exists in a world of spiritual reality."[21]

Tozer compiled and introduced the verse in this book and bundled it off to Christian Publications in early 1963. In the meantime, he continued his demanding travels, speaking at more conferences in the early 1960s than he had ever managed before. All the while he faithfully wrote editorials for *The Alliance Monthly*, fulfilled his duties with the national leadership team of the C&MA, and prepared two sermons a week in his role as preaching minister of Avenue Road Church.

* * * * * * * *

Dr. Tozer was hired with the understanding that he serve as a preacher and teacher, without the responsibilities of an ordinary pastor. These duties he gladly left in the hands of his associates, but the preacher/writer did not turn a blind eye to the flock. Like Ada, Aiden had always been alert to the marginalized, and when they relocated to Toronto this habit did not change. Indeed, one man in particular, a widower named Leonard Odam, attended morning and evening services every Sunday and eagerly listened to the Yankee preacher's words. Aiden noticed that Mr. Odam usually sat alone near the front, with no one in particular even noticing him. During their first year in Toronto, Aiden urged Ada to invite Odam to sit next to her so that he would not be so lonely. Always on the outlook for forlorn souls herself, she joined her husband in urging Leonard to sit with her at the front near the pulpit, inasmuch as each of them worshiped regularly without benefit of family companionship.

* * * * * * * *

By spring 1963 Ada and Aiden were beginning to feel at home in Canada. Although Aiden traveled more than ever, he was at least home almost every weekend. The peripatetic preacher had a heavy speaking schedule set for 1963, with engagements booked in New York, Ontario, and Oregon for the summer, plus other conference appearances for autumn and winter.

Ada's routine included regular missionary prayer meetings each week, and she utilized friends with cars as well as Toronto's ample public transportation to make her pastoral care calls at hospitals and to homes of shut-ins. Aiden rode buses and streetcars, too, but he also had a few young ministers and interns who happily drove him around in return for free lunches and many hours of conversation about books and how to develop a vital relationship with the Lord. Among these young Toronto men mentored by Dr. Tozer was Keith A. Price, who later became a well-known preacher and evangelist. Tozer took Price in tow and, "more than anyone else," Price said, "showed me how to quench that thirst" for God. "On learning I had no formal Bible training he encouraged me saying, 'To serve God you need neither a title, an office or a business card.'" Price recalled that one day he asked Tozer if he should go back to school because he "left school at fourteen." Tozer replied: "Young man, you have a hunger for God. You are busily engaged teaching the Word. In my observation, many like you who go back to finish their education never regain the momentum they had. Keep on pursuing God on your own." Tozer admitted that he himself had left school at age fourteen and never returned. "But you and I have one thing going for us: we _know_ we don't know, so we keep on trying to find out."[22]

Life in Toronto proved to be similar to life in Chicago for the Tozers. To be sure, Ada had more freedom for her visitation and prayer ministry because the children were gone. And, while Aiden had fewer responsibilities as a pastor in Canada, he seems to have devoted little if any more of his newfound freedom to his wife of forty-five years. Prayer, preaching, writing, travel, and mentoring young men took up most of his hours, leaving no time to develop the marital intimacy that they had both learned to live without.

To the people at Avenue Road Church in Toronto, Dr. and Mrs. Tozer appeared to be a happily married couple. And, on one level, they were. After decades of faithfully walking together in their separate worlds of existence, they had found a relatively comfortable level of accommodation.

Early on Sunday morning, May 12, the routine of life together in Toronto abruptly changed. Aiden experienced strong chest pains, Ada called a doctor, and he was placed in the hospital for observation. Ada spent several hours with him on Sunday, but at his insistence, she returned home that night to rest while he anticipated a good night's sleep before the battery of tests scheduled for Monday morning.

At 12:45 a.m. the preaching minister of Avenue Road Church briefly awakened with the knife-like pain of a coronary thrombosis. Within a few moments he passed through the veil of earth and met his beloved Savior face-to-face.

A memorial service was held in Toronto on May 15. Another one took place in Chicago two days later. Dr. A. W. Tozer was buried in Chicago, but in 1976 Ada had his earthly remains moved and buried with her family in a little Presbyterian Church cemetery at Ellet, Ohio near Akron.

Aiden W. Tozer had turned sixty-six less than a month before his death. Ada was sixty-four. Now more alone than ever, she had little money in the bank. Never having known about the family finances, she learned upon Aiden's death that he had routinely given half of his salary back to the church every month. Furthermore, he had eschewed seeking the provisions provided by the C&MA to build up a pension fund, and he had signed an agreement with Christian Publications in 1959 that relinquished his rights to royalties on paperback editions of *Pursuit of God*, *Root of the Righteous*, and *Born after Midnight*—his biggest-selling books with that publisher.

To the credit of the executives of the Christian and Missionary Alliance, the pension fund Dr. Tozer could have accrued was appropriated and given to his widow. At the final accounting she had $5,000 in life insurance and $7,000 in savings, counting the pension monies.[23]

◊　◊　◊　◊　◊　◊　◊　◊　◊

A. W. Tozer left his wife little monetary security, but he had encouraged her to reach out to Leonard Odam. Not one of these people—Leonard, Aiden, or Ada—could have foreseen or imagined the long-term effect of this Sunday morning relationship.

During the months after Dr. Tozer's death Ada and Leonard saw each another at church and visited socially. He had been widowed several years, and he was nearly ten years her senior. They both loved God and had been loving and loyal to their spouses. Now they found unbounded joy in being together. A year after

Aiden's death they married. The newlyweds drove to West Virginia for their honeymoon and spent several days in the home of one of Ada's closest Toronto friends who had moved from Canada to West Virginia in 1962. Ethel Wolfe recalled that the Odams spent their honeymoon at "her mother's house." Ethel and her family "decorated the bedroom the newlyweds were staying in and made big deal of it." Ethel and her mother put "up triangular streamers, like those used at grand openings of stores, all over the bedroom."[24]

For ten years Ada and Leonard enjoyed life together. From all accounts, including her letters to friends, this second marriage brought Ada fulfillment, joy, and a sense of freedom she hadn't experienced before. She took Leonard Odam's name and began signing letters "Ada Cecelia Odam." Exuding independence, one of her first acts of liberation was learning to drive Leonard's automobile. For the first time in her life she shook free from the bondage of depending upon other people or public transportation to get about town.

During the years 1964 to 1974 several people who were close to Ada lovingly inquired about her happiness. Her responses were consistent: "I have never been happier in my life. Aiden loved Jesus Christ, but Leonard Odam loves me."[25]

8

"If My Fire Is Not Large It Is Yet Real"

Legacy

It is nearly a half century since A. W. Tozer's death, and these years provide enough perspective to allow at least a preliminary assessment of his legacy. Any candid portrait of this twentieth-century prophet and Christian mystic reveals that he was far from perfect. Indeed, even after his conversion, growth in grace, and years of mature and successful ministry, personal flaws are readily apparent. That he consistently wounded his sensitive and loyal wife, albeit unintentionally, is irrefutable. That he revealed more of himself to a few young men he mentored than to his own children—with the possible exception of his daughter Rebecca—is undeniable. That he offended some members of his church and a few fellow ministers—but without malicious intent—is abundantly clear.

Looking back after several decades, however, reveals some significant evidence. First, all seven of Tozer's children became solid Christians and not one of them carried bitterness in their heart toward their father. Each one became relatively successful by the world's standards and functioned quite well in society, and they all expressed gratitude to God for their mother and father and with good reason. Besides being amply fed, clothed, and taught to worship God and respect all people, all seven children were strongly encouraged by both parents to get as much education as they could. This is remarkable considering that neither Ada nor Aiden had the opportunity to even finish high school, and furthermore, there was a strong strain of anti-intellectualism among many fundamentalists and evangelicals in the early and middle twentieth century. Thanks to unflagging parental encouragement, five of the children became college graduates and three earned advanced degrees from distinguished universities: Lowell (PhD in American Studies, University of Minnesota); Forrest (doctorate in law, University of Chicago); and Stanley (doctorate in pastoral counseling, Mead Seminary, University of Chicago).

In retrospect it is to Ada's credit that she accepted her pain with dignity and a spirit of marked charity. Because of her devotion to her husband and children, only a few people knew her grief; and half of those who did know, inferred it from observation rather than hearing it firsthand. A Christian woman who chose her words carefully, Ada Tozer had long before learned not to indulge in gossip. In the final analysis, she spoke glowingly of Aiden's accomplishments for the glory of God and the furtherance of His Kingdom, and even endearingly had his mortal remains removed from Chicago and placed among the graves of her beloved family in an Ohio cemetery. There is no evidence that she ever said so, but she must have treasured some satisfaction in knowing that A. W. Tozer could never have accomplished what he did without her personal and prayerful concern for him, their children, and the people of each local church they served.

Beyond the legacy of a godly immediate family, A. W. Tozer left in his wake a multitude of young men and women who gratefully maintained that his sermons, articles, and books strengthened their walk with Christ. Many young missionaries testified that Tozer was the man God used to call them to full-time ministry. Dr. H. Wilbert Norton, former president of Trinity College, Trinity Evangelical Divinity School, and later dean of Wheaton College Graduate School, said that "thousands of Christians heard his lucid application of Scripture . . . in six of the first eight Mid-America Keswick Conventions." Norton said "college and university students loved him," and at the 1954 InterVarsity missionary convention at the University of Illinois, he addressed "thousands of students." His message on "The Man God Uses" quickened hundreds on "dedication to God's will and missionary program for the world." Norton also said that Tozer's messages and writings "brought a new respect to many evangelicals of the place of the mind in Christian living," and "he also helped the intellectuals . . . see the place of piety as an expression of mind and heart."[1]

Dr. William Culbertson, the president of Moody Bible Institute and a man with widespread influence among evangelicals, also spoke at Tozer's memorial service in Chicago and eulogized his friend with these words:

> His ministry to me, both as between ourselves and in his public service, is a treasure I shall remember. The Lord gave Dr. Tozer many gifts. As God's servant, he was faithful in the human side of the talents God gave. Best of all, he knew the presence and power of the Spirit of God.[2]

Tozer's close friend J. Francis Chase acknowledged that, except for A. B. Simpson, no one person had done more than A. W. Tozer to help the Christian and Missionary Alliance spread the gospel, plant churches, and send and support missionaries throughout the world. There is no way to quantify the lasting effects of such ministry. But equally important, according to Chase, was Tozer's personal passion for the Lord Jesus Christ and his concomitant ability to encourage others to know Christ and to love Him more. "He was never so effective in his preaching as when he spoke on the wonders of his transcendent Lord," said Chase. "No passing theological fancy or fad engaged his powers. He had but one consuming passion. It was the pursuit of God Himself." Chase remembered that Tozer "would often say . . . 'God is easy to live with.'"[3]

⸭　⸭　⸭　⸭　⸭　⸭　⸭　⸭　⸭

A careful survey of Tozer's sermons and articles from the 1920s until his death in 1963 reveals a subtle shift in emphasis. Early in his preaching career he did the work of a traditional evangelist—presenting Christ crucified and resurrected, and then calling people to confess sins and repent. Along with his heart to reach lost souls, Tozer carried a burden to see revival break out in North America. His messages were strikingly prophetic and they speak to the early twenty-first century as surely as they spoke to his times. Tozer confronted errant Christian leaders. As one man said, "He was a voice in the wilderness of dead orthodoxy, defunct liberalism, and defeatist neo-orthodoxy."[4] He called saints and sinners alike to repent and be converted.

All of these challenges were and remain pertinent and stirring. Tozer's enduring legacy, however, flows from his gradual understanding that the Christian church—both her leaders and her rank and file—would never be truly converted and revived until they acquired a biblical vision of the heavenly Father through His Son, the Lord Jesus Christ.

Herein lies Tozer's enduring legacy. His passion to know God is still contagious. A Pauline mystic with both feet firmly on earth and both eyes riveted in the Holy Scriptures, and a heart given to Christ, he wrote these words in 1948 in the preface to *The Pursuit of God*: "Others before me have gone much farther into holy mysteries than I have done, but if my fire is not large it is yet real, and there may be those who can light their candle at its flame."[5]

Many continue to catch the fire of Tozer's love for God. His books still sell well, and *The Pursuit of God* and *The Knowledge of the Holy* are read by more people who hunger for "something more" than during his lifetime. Only eternity will reveal the full extent and effect of Tozer's "Society of the Burning Heart."

Notes

Chapter 1: "I've Had a Lonely Life"

1. Interview of James F. Hay Sr. by D. Shepson, October 10, 1995.

2. See Lyle W. Dorsett, "Introduction" in *Tozer Speaks to Students* (1998), 19.

3. For examples of Tozer's prophetic messages see his sermons and articles in the appendices.

4. Interview of Harry Verploegh by L. Dorsett, September 27, 1996.

5. For an excellent and succinct critique of the market-driven church, see John Parker, "Guide for the Cineplexed," *Touchstone*, July/August 2006, 19–20. See Tozer's "Prayer of a Minor Prophet," reprinted in *The Alliance Witness*, January 1964.

6. Charles Hummell, *Fire in the Fireplace: Charismatic Renewal in the Nineties* (1993).

7. Oden has written a three-volume *Systematic Theology:* Volume One, *The Living God* (1987), Volume Two, *The Words of Life* (1989), Volume Three, *Life in the Spirit* (1992). See, for example, vol. three, vii.

Chapter 2: "A Deep Strain of the Country"

1. "The Blight of Hillbillyism in Religion," *Alliance Weekly*, October 13, 1954.

2. Battles File, Verploegh Papers.

3. The materials on Clearfield County and environs, the facts and events surrounding the Tozer, Weaver, and Jackson families, in the entire chapter (unless otherwise noted) come from the Battles File; Clearfield County archives; Jane Elling's article on A. W. Tozer in *The Progress*, a Clearfield and environs paper, dated February 26, 1993; and the biographies by Fant and Snyder. Data has also been selected from *Pennsylvania: A Guide to the Keystone State* (1940) published by the Writer's Program of the WPA. Pennsylvania U.S. Census data has been consulted as well.

4. Tozer, *Alliance Weekly*, October 13, 1954.

5. Ibid.

6. A typescript of Reminiscences of the Tozer family, given to Arlene J. Davis, daughter of Essie Tozer, by her mother, is the source of this and other anecdotes about the years in rural Pennsylvania.

7. A. W. Tozer sermon, "The Second Coming," Mahaffey Camp, 1957.

8. Essie's Reminiscences, 21.

9. Ada Odam to R. W. Battles, Battles File, letter dated August 1, 1978.

10. Letter to Lyle Dorsett from Jane Kenney, April 8, 1997.

11. Verploegh Papers, vol. 4, 28.

12. Essie's Reminiscences, 2–3.

13. Ibid., 3.

14. Unless otherwise noted, for the following pages on McGuffey and his influence I have relied upon Lewis Atherton, *Main Street on the Middle Border* (1954) and his use of Harvey C. Minnich, *William Holmes McGuffey and His Readers* (1936) and Richard D. Mosier, *Making the American Mind: Social and Moral Ideas in the McGuffey Readers* (1947).

15. Essie's Reminiscences, 5–6.

16. Lewis Atherton, *Main Street on the Middle Border*, 65.

17. Ibid., 67.

18. Ibid., 66–68.

19. Ibid., 69.

20. Essie's Reminiscences, 6, 7, 21, 22.

21. Quoted in Atherton, *Main Street*, 69.

22. James L. Snyder, *In Pursuit of God: The Life of A. W. Tozer* (1991), 25.

23. Essie's Reminiscences, 12.

24. Ibid., 29.

25. Ibid.

Chapter 3: "I Heard His Voice—Ever So Faintly"

1. Fred Shannon, *The Farmers Last Frontier*

2. Lyle W. Dorsett, *Billy Sunday and the Redemption of Urban America* (1991), 109–110.

3. U.S. Census Records

4. Snyder, *In Pursuit of God*, 33–34; Essie's Reminiscences, 30.

5. Snyder, *In Pursuit of God*, 34.

6. Essie's Reminiscences, 30.

7. Ibid.

8. Snyder, *In Pursuit of God*, 35.

9. Verploegh Papers.

10. Ibid.

11. Ibid.

12. Fant Jr., David J. *A. W. Tozer: A Twentieth-Century Prophet* (1964), 15.

13. Essie's Reminiscences, 31.

14. Verploegh Papers.

15. Essie's Reminiscences, 31.

16. Frank B. Miller to R. W. Battles, August 21, 1973, Battles File.

17. Some accounts say he was baptized in the Brethren Church (see Snyder, *In Pursuit of God*, 41). But the July 24, 1963 issue of *Alliance Witness*, p. 7, says Christian Church. It is possible he was baptized twice.

18. The dates he formally joined the Methodist Church and the Alliance Church are 1915 and 1916 respectively, according to p. 7 of *Alliance Witness*, July 24, 1963.

19. Ada Tozer Odam to R. W. Battles, July 21, 1973.

20. The background on Ada Pfautz comes from her letters to R.W. Battles (Battles File) and from chapter 4 in Snyder, *In Pursuit of God*. I also received much help from an interview with Rebecca Tozer Michaels, November 1, 2000.

21. Ada Tozer Odam to R. W. Battles, July 21, 1973. Ada slightly confused the dates in this letter. They were actually married on April 26, five days after Aiden's 21st birthday. I corrected the dates in the quotation.

22. A. W. Tozer, *Tragedy in the Church*, 37.

23. Ada Tozer Odam to R. W. Battles, July 21, 1973.

24. Ibid.

25. Ibid.

26. Ada Tozer Odam to R. W. Battles, no date.

27. Ibid.

Chapter 4: "I Got My First Awful, Wonderful, Entrancing Vision of God"

1. Ada Tozer Odam to R. W. Battles, August 5, 1973, Battles File.

2. Ibid.

3. Ibid.

4. John Keegan, *The First World War* (1999), chapter 10.

5. Tozer is listed in *The Official Roster of Ohio Soldiers, Sailors and Marines in the World War 1917–1918*. Records and clippings from the Chillocothe and Ross County Public Library contain much valuable material and photographs that reveal various aspects of camp life.

6. Ada Tozer Odam to R. W. Battles, August 5, 1973, Battles File.

7. Ibid.

8. A typical example of Tozer's celebrating his country roots with country people is a sermon, "The Second Coming" which he delivered at a Mahaffey Camp Meeting in 1957. Copy in author's personal collection.

9. F. Bertram Miller to R. W. Battles, September 17, 1973, Battles File.

10. Snyder, *In Pursuit of God*, 53–54 and Ada Tozer Odam to R. W. Battles, August 11, 1978, Battles File.

11. Ada Tozer Odam, August 11, 1978.

12. Ibid.

13. Ibid.

14. Dorsett interview with Raleigh Tozer, September 7, 2000. He said his mother always said she weighed 98 pounds until Raleigh was born in 1928, when she added 34 pounds that she never lost. A photo of her taken in West Virginia, in a file owned by the author, reveals her physique.

15. Dorsett interview with Rebecca Michaels, November 1, 2000.

16. This prayer was published in the *Alliance Weekly*, May 6, 1950, the first issue after Tozer became editor of this official C&MA publication.

17. Dorsett interview with Wendell Tozer, February 27, 1997.

18. Dorsett interview with Rebecca Michaels, November 1, 2000 and a letter from Ada Tozer Odam to R. W. Battles, August 1, 1978.

19. See Ada Tozer Odam's letters to Battles in the 1970s, in the author's files.

20. Ibid.

21.This general observation grew out of what I gleaned in oral history interviews with all seven of the Tozer children.

22. Stanley Tozer interview with Dorsett, October 19, 1999.

23. Wendell and Forrest Tozer told me this an interview February 27, 1997.

24. Verploegh Papers. Sermon file.

25. Stanley Tozer to Dorsett, October 19, 1999.

26. See, E. M. Perkins, *Fred Francis Bosworth: His Life Story* (1927) and C. D. Weaver's entry on Bosworth and B. Barons entry on J. A. Dowie, in D. G. Reid, et al., *Dictionary of Christianity in America* (1990).

27. Ibid.

28. A. E. Thompson, *The Life of A. B. Simpson* (1947) and A. W. Tozer, *Wingspread* (1943), Charles W. Nienkirchen, *A. B. Simpson and the Pentecostal Movement* (1992).

29. Lyle W. Dorsett, *A Passion for Souls: A Life of D. L. Moody*, (1997), chapter 11.

30. See, e.g., *The Light of Life*, vol. 1, January 1925.

31. H. P. Shelly, "Paul Daniel Rader" in Reid, et al., ed., *Dictionary of Christianity in America*.

32. Lyle W. Dorsett, *Billy Sunday and the Redemption of Urban America* (1991).

33. Much on Greenwald, Tozer, Bosworth, Shuman, and the Indianapolis Church is in vol. 1, *The Light of Life*, January 1925.

34. Harry Verploegh told me that this was A. W. Tozer's attitude at the Chicago church. And both Wendell and Forrest Tozer commented on their father's disdain for money and the hardship this put on their mother as she tried to feed a growing family.

35. See, e.g., vol 1., *The Light of Life*, January 1925.

36. Rolland later changed his name to Raleigh.

37. Dorsett interview with Raleigh Tozer, September 7, 2000.

Chapter 5: "It May Be a Good Thing I Never Went to Seminary"

1. This is testimony from Harry Verploegh who knew both Tozer and Chase personally. Several of Tozer's children, like Verploegh, told me that Chase was perhaps their father's closest friend and that he was extremely brilliant and never intimidated by Tozer's razor-sharp wit and mind.

2. J. F. Chase to R. W. Battles, July 1974, Battles File.

3. Snyder, *In Pursuit of God*, chapter 7.

4. Ibid., 75.

5. For background on Chicago as a training center for young people, see Lyle W. Dorsett, *A Passion for Souls: The Life of Dwight L. Moody* (1997).

6. Snyder, *In Pursuit of God*, 74–76.

7. For many years the Alliance claimed it was not a denomination, rather it was an alliance of Christians from many traditions who advocated the mobilization of people for evangelism, as well as home and foreign missions. By not meeting on Sunday morning, they avoided competing with other churches.

8. Chase to Battles, July 1974; Snyder, *In Pursuit of God*, 76.

9. Ibid.

10. Snyder, *In Pursuit of God*, 78.

11. Ibid.

12. Dorsett interview with Verploegh, March 26, 1997, and information from Lowell Tozer in 2007.

13. Catherine Sorich owned 10735 Prospect when I interviewed her in October 2006. A forty-year resident/owner of the house, she generously gave me a history of the property with detailed descriptions of rooms and additions.

14. Dorsett interview with Stanley Tozer, October 19, 1999. He had fond memories of the Sunday dinners with guests who were "poor people Mom invited."

15. Dorsett interview with Wendell and Forrest (Bud) Tozer, February 27, 1997; and an interview with Rebecca Tozer Michaels, November 1, 2000.

16. Dorsett interview with Verploegh, March 26, 1997.

17. An address by Ray McAfee, September 29, 1987, to a C&MA meeting. Copy in Dorsett's papers.

18. Verploegh told me this, and I found similar comments in an interview (Robert Henry with Ruby Huston: March 9, 1999).

19. McAfee, "Tozer Reflections."

20. Don Shepson interview with Bernard King, October 16, 1995.

21. Several of his children related this to me.

22. Sermon titled "Above All." This was delivered at Mahaffey Camp Meeting in 1957.

23. Dorsett interview with Forrest and Wendell Tozer, February 27, 1997.

24. See, for example, his comments in *Alliance Weekly*, July 1, 1944. This is typical of his view of methods designed to attract numbers. Also several people interviewed mentioned the fact that some people found him abrasive. This article and several similar pieces are reprinted in Appendix Two.

25. On several occasions Harry Verploegh explained Tozer's attitude to me. He also said some people did not like his refusal to greet the people when they left the church.

26. *Alliance Weekly*, May 31, 1941.

27. Ibid., January 22, 1944. The core of his teaching to teachers can be found summarized in this article and in *What's in the Bible That People Ought to Know About?*, a booklet distributed by Christian Publications.

28. Robert Henry interview with David Enlow, April 6, 1999.

29. See correspondence in Verploegh file.

30. Billy Graham to V. R. Edman, October 6, 1952. Edman Collection, Off Campus Box #2, Folder BGEA Correspondence, 1952–1959.

31. Don Shepson interview with G. Carlson, November 6, 1995.

32. Enlow interview, April 6, 1999.

33. Don Shepson interview with Mrs. Louis King, September 26, 1995.

34. Don Shepson interview with Louis King, September 26, 1995.

35. Lyle W. Dorsett, editor, *Tozer Speaks to Students* (1998), Introduction.

36. Ibid.

37. Verploegh to Dorsett, September 27, 1996.

38. The material related to the seven children and family life in general comes from my personal interviews with each: Lowell (September 7, 2000); Forrest (February 27, 1999); A. W., Jr. (May 21, 2001); Rolland (September 7, 2000); Wendell (February 27, 1999); Stanley (October 19, 1999); Rebecca (November 1, 2000).

39. Lowell Tozer to Dorsett, September 7, 2000.

40. Verploegh to Dorsett, February 27, 1997.

41. Raleigh Tozer to Dorsett, September 7, 2000.

42. Battles File, Verploegh Papers.

43. Forrest Tozer to Dorsett, February 27, 1997.

Chapter 6: "A Growing Hunger after God Himself"

1. Lowell Tozer to Dorsett, September 7, 2000.

2. I gleaned these insights from interviews with all seven Tozer children. Lowell commented on being taught to "love learning," September 7, 2000.

3. A. W. Tozer Jr., to Dorsett, May 21, 2000.

4. Lowell Tozer to Dorsett, September 7, 2000.

5. Interviews with Wendell, Lowell, Forrest, and Aiden informed these observations.

6. Chase quoted by James Snyder, *In Pursuit of God*, 97.

7. Ibid., 96–97.

8. Raleigh Tozer to Dorsett, September 7, 2000.

9. Bernard King to Don Shepson, October 16, 1995.

10. Chase manuscript, Battles File, November 1973.

11. Samuel M. Zwemer, "Introduction," *The Pursuit of God* (1948), 5–6. Tozer's own words are on p. 7.

12. Harry Verploegh provided this information in early 1997.

13. Clara Moore to Robert Henry, May 4, 1999.

14. Ibid.

15. See letters from Ada Tozer Odam to R. W. Battles, from 1973 and 1974.

16. Clara Moore to Robert Henry, May 4, 1999.

17. My primary source on Edman comes from Earle E. Cairns, *V. Raymond Edman: In the Presence of the King* (1972).

18. The articles appeared in *Christian Life* in May, August, October, and December 1957.

19. These addresses are published in Lyle W. Dorsett, editor, *Tozer Speaks to Students*, (1998).

20. *Christian Life*, August 1957.

21. Files on all of these services are in the author's personal collection.

22. My wife, Mary Dorsett, was archivist for Wheaton College's Buswell Library in the 1980s. Although I never examined the files, she mentioned the Graham reference to me and she also found copies of eleven sermons Tozer preached at Wheaton in the 1950s.

23. J. Julius Scott to Dorsett, May 1, 1997.

24. Bernard King to Don Shepson, October 16, 1995. I also met and talked to Dr. King in November 1990.

25. See *Alliance Weekly* notices in July and August 1937; May 15, 1949; March 4, 1950; and December 1958.

26. Quoted in *The Alliance Witness*, July 24, 1963, 13.

27. Robert G. Flood and Jerry B. Jenkins, *Teaching the World, Reaching the World* (1985), 72–73.

28. Quoted in *The Alliance Witness*, July 24, 1963, 13.

29. David J. Fant, *A. W. Tozer: A Twentieth-Century Prophet* (1964), refers to Tozer's "Society" of young people of similar heart on p. 147. The precise origin of the phrase "Society of the Burning Heart" is claimed by numerous mid-twentieth-century people. Tozer himself used the phrase "Children of the Burning Heart" in *The Pursuit of God*, 10.

30. The following paragraphs, unless otherwise noted, come from interviews with Harry Verploegh in the late 1990s, a 20-page "Reflection" on Tozer that McAfee prepared in 1987 (a copy in Dorsett's paper given by Verploegh), and an article written for the periodical *Power for Living* by McAfee given to the author by Jim Adair, the editor of *Power* and an acquaintance of Tozer and McAfee.

31. Clara Moore to Robert Henry, May 4, 1999.

32. Raymond McAfee in the article from *Power* cited in note 30.

33. Ibid.

34. McAfee's "Reflection" cited in note 30.

35. Edman, *They Found the Secret*.

36. Clara Moore to Robert Henry, May 4, 1999.

37. Ira Gerig to Robert Henry, February 20, 1999.

38. Gerald Smith to Don Shepson, December 11, 1995.

39. Gordon Cathey to Dorsett, October 4, 2004.

40. Ed J. Maxey to Lyle Dorsett, June 6, 1997.

41. Ibid.

42. "A Word in Season," *Alliance Weekly*, July 1, 1944.

43. A. W. Tozer to Union Gospel Press, April 11, 1956. Copy in Verploegh Papers given to author.

44. *Alliance Weekly*, March 30, 1946 and May 11, 1946.

45. Ira Gerig to Robert Henry, May 4, 1999.

46. "A Word in Season," March 10, 1945.

47. Sermon titled "The Word," delivered at Mahaffey Camp, July 28, 1951.

48. Published by Christian Publications (no date) under this title in the 1950s: *The Menace of the Religious Movie*.

49. Ibid., 3.

50. Aiden W. Tozer Jr. to Lyle Dorsett, May 21, 2001.

51. Interviews: Verploegh with Dorsett, March 26, 1997; Gerald Smith with Don Shepson, December 11, 1995; Bernard King with D. Shepson, October 16, 1995.

52. Rebecca Tozer Michaels to Dorsett, November 1, 2000. The following paragraphs, unless otherwise noted, came from this interview.

53. Harry Verploegh, as well as several of Ada's children, mentioned her freedom to minis-

ter and her delight in doing it.

54. R. S. Brown to Robert Henry, May 24, 1999.

55. Mrs. Louis King to Don Shepson, September 28, 1995.

56. Ethel Wolfe to Robert Henry, April 9, 1999.

57. James Hoy to Don Shepson, October 10, 1995.

Chapter 7: "I Do Not Believe There Is Any Color Line in the Kingdom of God"

1. See Tozer's sermons and articles in the appendix for examples of his convictions.

2. R. W. Battles is one of the many who mentioned Tozer's sensitivity to beggars and other hurting people.

3. Harry Verploegh to Dorsett in several conversations at his home in 1997.

4. Eleanor Howell to Tozer, December 10, 1958, copies form a collection of correspondence given to the author by Harry Verploegh.

5. Ibid., Tozer to Howell, December 12, 1958.

6. Ibid., Helen Epperson to Tozer, February 11, 1959.

7. Ibid., Melvin Leidig to Tozer, March 25, 1959.

8. William Tuttle, *Race Riot in Chicago in the Red Summer of 1919* (1970); Allan Spear, *Black Chicago: The Making of a Negro Ghetto, 1890–1920* (1967).

9. John Hope Franklin, *From Slavery to Freedom: A History of Negro Americans* (Third Edition, 1967), 610.

10. Chase's *Reminiscences* in the R. W. Battles Collection, 4.

11. Ibid., 5.

12. Quoted in Snyder, *In Pursuit of God*, 217.

13. Ibid., 216–217.

14. Ibid., 217.

15. Ibid., 218.

16. Ibid., 218–219.

17. Ibid., 219–220.

18. Foreword by A. W. Tozer, 1.

19. *The Pursuit of God*, preface, 7.

20. *The Knowledge of the Holy*, vii and subtitle of the book.

21. *The Christian Book of Mystical Verse* (1963), v–vi.

22. Keith A. Price, "Thirsting after God," *Alliance Life*, April 9, 1997.

23. Royalty Agreement is in a file labeled "Royalties/Contract." And other details come from Ada Tozer's correspondence in 1976 and 1977 with R. W. Battles. These documents are in the author's possession.

24. Ethel Wolfe to Robert Henry, April 9, 1999.

25. Harry Verploegh's wife, Ethel Wolfe's mother, and at least two of the Tozer children reported the same response. I learned this from oral history interviews with Verploegh, Wolfe, and Wendell and Forrest Tozer.

Chapter 8: "If My Fire Is Not Large It Is Yet Real"

1. Norton's address at the Tozer Memorial Service in Chicago, printed in *The Alliance*

Witness, July 24, 1963, 13.

2. See *The Alliance Witness*, July 24, 1963, 13.

3. Ibid., 2, and similar insights appear in Chase's letters to R. W. Battles written in the 1970s, now in possession of the author.

4. Quoted by H. W. Norton, *Alliance Witness*, July 24, 1963, 13.

5. *The Pursuit of God*, 10. Serious students of Tozer's mysticism should read E. Lynn Harris, *The Mystic Spirituality of A. W. Tozer, A Twentieth-Century American Protestant* (1992).

A Note on Sources

Much of this book is based upon previously untapped primary sources, in particular, thirty-six oral history interviews that either I or one of my research assistants conducted. Especially helpful were the interviews that I personally conducted with all seven of the Tozer children and Harry Verploegh, one of Tozer's closest friends.

Harry Verploegh gave me his extensive files of Tozer materials, including typescript reminiscences written by Francis Chase and Essie Tozer, as well as a large collection of original letters and documents collected by R. W. Battles, who had hoped to write a biography of Dr. Tozer. The Battles collection included personal letters replete with family lore from Ada Tozer Odam, as well as other materials she gave to Battles to help him with his projected biography.

My personal collection of the *Alliance Weekly* (later the *Alliance Witness*) for the forty years Tozer was in ministry with the Christian and Missionary Alliance is an invaluable resource. This periodical tracks his speaking engagements and carries numerous articles and editorials he wrote.

Statistics relating to the communities where the Tozers lived come from official U. S. Census statistics, as well as from data compiled by various state and local agencies.

A.W. Tozer's original sermons have been an invaluable resource. The collections preserved by Ruth Ranshaw, as well as the collection of broadcasts preserved by the Moody Bible Institute's radio station (WMBI) have been extremely helpful.

The two previously published biographies of Tozer—David J. Fant, *A. W. Tozer: A Twentieth Century Prophet* (1964) and James L. Snyder, *In Pursuit of God: The Life of A. W. Tozer* (1991)—are important books that proved to be quite helpful.

Finally, the serious reader should consult the endnotes for each chapter inasmuch as they reveal a host of other primary and secondary sources that have been relied upon by the author.

A Bibliography of A. W. Tozer's Works

Books available through Wingspread Publishers, Camp Hill, PA

The Attributes of God, Volume I

The Attributes of God, Volume I Journal

The Attributes of God, Volume II

The Best of A. W. Tozer, Volume 1

The Best of A. W. Tozer, Volume 2

Born after Midnight

The Christian Book of Mystical Verse

Christ the Eternal Son

The Counselor

The Early Tozer: A Word in Season

Echoes from Eden

Faith Beyond Reason

Gems from Tozer

God Tells the Man Who Cares

How to be Filled with the Holy Spirit

I Call It Heresy!

I Talk Back to the Devil

Jesus, Author of Our Faith

Jesus Is Victor

Jesus, Our Man in Glory

Let My People Go, a biography of Robert A. Jaffray

Man: The Dwelling Place of God

Men Who Met God

The Next Chapter after the Last

Of God and Men

Paths to Power

The Price of Neglect

The Pursuit of God

The Pursuit of God: A 31-Day Experience

The Pursuit of Man (formerly The Divine Conquest)

The Quotable Tozer

The Quotable Tozer II

The Radical Cross

Renewed Day by Day, Volume 1

Renewed Day by Day, Volume 2

The Root of the Righteous

Rut, Rot or Revival

The Set of the Sail

The Size of the Soul

Success and the Christian

That Incredible Christian

This World: Playground or Battleground?

The Tozer CD-Rom Library

Tozer on the Almighty God

Tozer on Christian Leadership

Tozer on the Holy Spirit

Tozer on Worship and Entertainment

The Tozer Pulpit (in two volumes)

Tozer Speaks to Students

Tozer Topical Reader

Tragedy in the Church: The Missing Gifts

The Warfare of the Spirit

We Travel an Appointed Way

Whatever Happened to Worship?

Who Put Jesus on the Cross?

Wingspread, a biography of A. B. Simpson

Books available with other publishers

Harper One:
The Knowledge of the Holy

Zondervan:
Keys to the Deeper Life

Bridge-Logos:
A. W. Tozer: Fellowship of the Burning Heart

Appendix One

Restoring Dignity to Christian Worship

"A Word in Season"
Alliance Weekly, July 1, 1944

Perhaps I am growing conservative now that I am well past that time when life is said to begin, but whatever the reason, I confess myself very much distressed of the persistence among religious people of that condition which, for lack of a name, I shall call the Hollywood mentality.

I had been naïve enough to believe that we had been disillusioned by the sorry performances of the personality boys of a few years ago, and that we had recovered from that form of abnormal psychology which we caught from the movies; but evidently I was too optimistic. Like malaria it's back on us again.

How does the disease work? It distorts the vision so that the victim cannot discern true values in the work of the Lord. He shrugs off impatiently the time-honored ways of the saints and goes out for color, flash, size, vim, and zip. Quiet trust, stability, repose: these are passed up in a flurry of religious excitement.

Numbers come first, so anything will do if it will bring a

crowd. The most dismal example to come to my notice the shoddy means used to coax in a crowd appeared on the church page of a big city daily recently: "7:30 P.M., Moving Pictures of Cannibalism." And they were advertising a missionary convention!

The fevered prophets who promote this highly nervous variant of true Christianity long for publicity as a fever patient thirsts for water. It is their life. Their shameless clamor after press notice is evidence enough of their lush carnality, and nobody knows it better than the sarcastic newsmen who have to handle the copy.

Even in some of the best spiritual circles where symptoms are less marked, there is still too much evidence of this disease. Pulpit committees demand "big" names for their services; and when they are forced sometimes to put up with a humble and obscure servant of the Lord, they sit disappointed and uncomfortable, wondering nervously what the public will think of their man.

Compared with the spirit and teaching of the New Testament, this whole attitude is seen to be unbelieving and earthly, and the results can only be tragic at last.

"A Plea for Christian Dignity"
Alliance Weekly, March 30, 1946

There is about the Holy Spirit a dignity which is inherent in His nature and which imparts itself in some measure to every soul wherein He dwells.

By *dignity* is meant not pomposity nor snobbishness, but what the dictionary calls "elevation of character; nobleness or formal reserve of manner, aspect or style; loftiness and grace." This so perfectly describes the person of our Lord Jesus that one would almost guess that the lexicographer had had Him in mind when he wrote it. Such elevation of character springs from a high estimate of one's own worth in God, a preoccupation with heavenly things, a good conscience, and a heart full of pure love.

Sweet dignity has always been a mark of the true saint. They have had about them a certain severity of manner, a kindly aloofness which discouraged familiarity but which inspired boundless confidence and drew to them the serious minded and the troubled in heart.

In his exquisite "Deserted Village" Goldsmith describes the country pastor of old English times, and his description puts to shame the snappy personality boys who abound in modern pulpits. A simple man he was, this rustic shepherd, "and passing rich with forty pounds a year," but his innate force of character lifted him far above the plain surroundings amid which he toiled, and gave to his life a grandeur above the majesty of potentates and kings.

> "At church, with meek and unaffected grace,
> His looks adorned the venerable place.
> His ready smile a parent's warmth exprest,
> Their welfare pleased him and their cares distrest.
> To them his heart, his love, his griefs were given,
> But all his serious thoughts had rest in heaven.
> As some tall cliff that lifts its awful form,
> Swells from the vale and midway leaves the storm,
> Though round its breasts the rolling clouds are spread,
> Eternal sunshine settles on its head."

Protestantism lost a glory (or revealed that it no longer had it) when we began to call our ministers by their nicknames, when indeed we found that we *could* do so. When "Billy," "Bob" and "Bud" came into the pulpit, respect for the clergy went out. Our effort to prove to the carnal and sin-loving public that the gospel preacher is a "real fellow," no different from other men except that he has "taken Jesus," has resulted in a distinct lowering of the esteem in which the man of God had once been held. The confused and muddled world is likely to take us pretty much at our own value. If our opinion of ourselves and the intrinsic worth of our own lives is not high enough to keep from being vulgar, the world will accept our judgment and treat us accordingly. But the loss to both the Church and the world is beyond all counting.

The vulgarity of some fundamentalists is a real tragedy for the dying world. No one with an ounce of sincerity wants to trust his or her soul to a religious clown, and in many places the only religionists who still preserve the solemnity of their profession are the modernists and the priests. This, rather than an unwillingness to follow Christ, may account for the wholesale shift on the part of the populace from orthodoxy to liberalism and from Protestantism to the Catholic Church. Nothing is easier for us than to alibi ourselves out of this and to put the blame on the higher critic, but I for one do not feel that all the fault lies there. Loss of public confidence may be at the bottom of it.

Our basic levity of spirit is revealed by our language, our music, and our worship. Much of our modern religious advertising reflects the same fault. Imagine if you can a newspaper "ad" written by one of the snappy gospeleers of our day announcing a meeting by Charles G. Finney. It would in all likelihood run something after this fashion:

> Here's what you've been waiting for!
> Presenting Chas. G. (Chuck) Finney
> Amazing revival star
> Sharp at 8:00
> "Chuck" will give out with some thrilling talk.
> He preaches—but good.
> Also featured will be Rev. Daniel (Dan) Nash.
> Old "Bent-knee" Nash in person.
> Positively the keenest intercessor to appear
> before an American audience.
> He once prayed with a president.

Perhaps in writing this I am guilty of the very thing I deplore. If any justification for it exists, it is that I have seen this kind of advertising in scores of city newspapers. A think like that is too horrible to contemplate without pain, and indeed nothing like it could have happened where such a man as Finney was involved. One look at the Spirit-filled revivalist and the "ad" writer would have shrunk back discomfited. The man of God would have blasted such tawdry boasting out of the world. He would never have permitted himself to be made a fool of in that fashion. Too bad many of our modern evangelists not only allow such swelling talk about themselves, but appear actually to take delight in it.

The nervous desire for "contacts" found everywhere in religious circles is another symptom of the same abject poverty of life. The lonely solitudes seldom hear now the cry of a Moses or an Elijah. These have forsaken the mountain and the desert and are now haunting cafeterias, making contacts for the gospel. Schopenhauer said, "The more a man is in himself, the less he will want from other people—the less, indeed, other people can be to him. This is why a high degree of intellect tends to make a man unsocial." If "a high degree of intellect" were changed to "a high degree of spirituality" the saying would still be true. "The greatest saints," said Thomas à Kempis, "avoided the society of men when they could conveniently, and did rather choose to live to God in secret. He therefore that intends to attain to the more inward and spiritual things of religion must with Jesus depart from the multitude and press of the people." One of Wesley's biographers said of him, "He lived habitually with God, and only came down at stated times to speak to the people."

There can be no doubt that most of us talk too much for our own good. We call it "fellowship," but the results are seldom beneficial, often bad. The usual effect of religious shop talk is to vitiate the spirit and impair the inward life. "As often as I have been among men, I have returned home less a man than I was before." This has been the testimony of hundreds of earnest Christians. In the dark hours of persecution when the people of God are few and scattered, how sweet has been the communion of saints. "Then they that feared the Lord spake often one to another: and the Lord hearkened, and heard it, and a book of remembrance was written before him for them that feared the Lord, and that thought upon his name." That is one thing. Cheap familiarity and carnal loquacity are quite another.

We should remember, however, that true Christian dignity is a quality of mind which follows long communion with God and continual preoccupation with heavenly verities. It cannot be imitated. Levity of character is proof of a narrowness of heart. Paul cried out to the Corinthians, "Ye are straightened in your own bowels. Be ye also enlarged." An enlarged heart will cure cheapness of soul. Commonness and light familiarity cannot long keep company with the Holy Ghost, nor with the man in whom He makes His blessed habitation.

To sum it all up, our real need is inward riches. <u>We need to learn how to be still and know that God is God.</u> <u>We need to "practice the presence of God" till we take on something of the nobility of our divine Companion.</u> <u>We need to cultivate silence and discover the riches of the secret places.</u> <u>We need to discover God in the deeps of our own souls.</u>

The Church of God needs prophets, the kind of prophets that are bred of the silence and the long contemplations. Such prophets will not be easy companions; they will not be jolly fellows with a "testimony for Jesus." They will be serious men whose eyes look far; and though they may be meek and lowly as the Lord whom they adore, there will be about them a suggestion of royalty, a noble reserve of bearing that cannot be mistaken. And if there is hope for the Church before Christ returns, that how will lie with such men as these.

Appendix Two

The Decline of Godly Leadership

"The Decline in Godly Leadership"
Alliance Weekly, May 11, 1946

The active leadership of the gospel wing of the Church in America has in recent years largely passed out of the hands of men of solid Christian character, and has gone over into the control of young men who are remarkable neither for their learning nor their godliness, but who possess a flair for publicity, boundless ambition, and a pretty fair talent for successful promotion. Gravity has been pushed aside to make place for cleverness, and the novice is now in the saddle in direct violation of the solemn warning of the Apostle Paul.

No Spiritual Giants

The giants of the Kingdom who lived and wrought a generation or two ago are now gone home. While they lived among us, they led the Church by the sheer power of their gifts and the admitted superiority of their personal characters. But, strange as it may be, while they themselves were might men and men of renown, they were not able to sire a spiritual progeny equal to themselves, so that, as they left us one after one, their mantles fell upon men very much inferior to them in ability, learning, and piety. The generation now in charge consists of the sons and grandsons of the old spiritual heroes, and great has been the decline from year to year.

Though it may seem a gloomy conclusion, we must assume either that the race of spiritual giants is now extinct within the borders of evangelical orthodoxy, or that, if some do exist, they are for some reason strangely articulate, for it is hardly an uncharitable deduction that spiritual greatness is not discoverable in the lives and labors of our modern gospel propagandists.

One of the woes pronounced upon Israel at one time was that their princes should be children. God said that He would take away from Jerusalem and from Judah the mighty man, the judge, the prophet, the prudent and the ancient, the honorable man and the counselor, and would give children to be their princes and make babes to rule over them. However much it may be deplored, it is yet not a singular nor uncommon thing for the more worthy to be led by the less worthy, for it is often true that the mighty in a given field are silent while the quasi-great are loud in their outcries. Of course, the public, being neutral, will usually follow the most persistent voice. Plato said that the penalty good men pay for failure to take part in politics is to be ruled over by bad men. Sound, God-honoring believers in our day have to a large degree surrendered their leadership to lesser men who are not their equal in godliness but who are hungry for power and so are ready to take over at the first opportunity.

Unworthy Programs

Many of our latter day gospel programs bear a disturbing similarity to the familiar radio show. All the elements are there: The sponsor, the product, the artists, the show, and the commercials. The sponsor who is assumed to be back of it all is the Lord; the product is the gospel; the "artists" are the various stars of the evangelistic firmament both speakers and singers; the show is the demonstration these stars put on for the amusement of the public; and the commercial is the dutiful plug which is introduced every so often in favor of the Lord and the gospel. The whole thing is a fair imitation of a soap opera. The discriminating listener is left with the feeling that the artist has a following altogether apart from his sponsor, and that if he were to switch sponsors, his fans would simply switch with him and go right on enjoying the program.

Brethren, these things ought not so to be. The true witness has no "act" apart from his Lord. His act is to reveal his Lord. He will have no acceptance where his Lord is rejected, and he is accepted only as and where his Lord is welcomed. Samuel was rejected from ruling over Israel, but only after Israel had first rejected God.

Uncompromising Leaders

The need today is for leaders identified so fully with the cross-carrying Jesus that they have no life apart from Him, no ambition except to make Him appear glorious in the sight of men. Such as these will seek no place, no reputation. Christ Himself will be their glory and their all.

He is a poor and wretched example of a Christian who will accept a seat at a banquet where his Lord is not welcome, who will bask in the sunshine of a friendship which his Lord cannot share. The true servant will ask nothing better than to be where Jesus is, to stand or fall with Him in the favor of men, to suffer or rejoice with Him at all times.

At a time like this every real Christian must make his decision, whether he shall drift along with the religious times, weakly going wherever the noisy promoters take him, or whether he shall stand to resist the movements which tend away from the sound and solid teachings of spiritual religion. The Christian with spiritual vision and courage to follow it will not take long hesitate which course to take. He will set his house in order and prepare to bear his cross along with his Saviour.

Unproved Movements

Right here is the place to discuss the matter of various movements and organizations which are springing up these days like grass in the back pasture. What should be the attitude of the God-honor-ing Christian toward these many clamorous bidders for his support and loyalty? The answer cannot be given in one sentence, and yet it is not hard to find our bearings if we but have a little independence of judgment and courage to stand alone.

A few such organizations there are which can command the re-spect of the Christian public and are for that reason worthy of our support. But for the most part the many organizations which are springing into bloom here and there are no more than visible evi-dence of fear on the part of some and ambition on the part of others. The ambitious will lead and the timid will follow. The result is a multiplicity of overlapping groups consuming millions of dollars each year to keep up offices and pay salaries for the carrying on of projects which it is morally certain God never started. From all such we are in duty bound to turn away.

Every movement that solicits our support should be put to the test of sound Christian godliness. We have a perfect right to ask to see its credentials before we cast in our lot with it. We are, in fact, commanded in the inspired Word to do so, and we disobey God when we fail. We should ask first: Who is the hero of the piece, Christ or some star of the religious firmament? Next, are they who guide the project saintly and self-denying men whose records show them to be wholly concerned with the honor of God? Is there evi-dence of the travail of the Holy Ghost in the movement, or was it born painlessly at a get-together luncheon somewhere? Is there any real need for the organization, or is it a duplication of already exist-ing means of accomplishing the same thing? Will our money, if we pay it into their treasuries, be used to spread the message of dying love and to encourage believers to seek to be Christlike? Will we be assisting men and women to live in all meekness of humility, to study to mind their own business, to live godly at home and attend to their duties as pilgrims of eternity, or will we be giving to the sup-port of overpaid men who know not what sacrifice means? Will we be promoting the personal glory of publicity-hungry men or truly supporting the work of the Holy Ghost in this generation?

Before we join any religious parades we had better pause and find out where they are going. We must all appear before the judgment seat of Christ soon or late to receive the things done in the body. Now we have opportunity to call our shots. It will be too late then.

The Appeal of the Christlike

It may be justly said that the writer of these lines is of all men the least worthy to call Jesus Lord or to speak in His sinless Name. Amen. So be it. Nevertheless I have a soul to save, a God to glorify, and no one can stand sponsor for me before the great assize. There I must stand alone; and if it should be necessary that I stand alone for a little while here, I shall not wish it had been otherwise when the day comes. If my fellowship is worth asking then it will be given to the saintly man, the humble man, and the holy. He who would call me to his side must have garments that smell of myrrh and loes and cassia out of the ivory palaces. Let him show me his scars and then command my service. I shall not withhold it. Gladly will I toil beside the man who reminds me of my Saviour. As for the others, let them not trouble me. I am trying to show forth the glory of Him who called me out of darkness into His marvelous light. It is a great work and I cannot come down.

Hear two powerful messages from A.W. Tozer for **FREE** at www.tozerpulpit.com

The first is a sermon titled "The Kingdom of God Lies Not in Words, but in Power" delivered on Sunday morning June 16, 1957, at the Southwest Alliance Church in Chicago, Illinois.

The second is his last recorded public address, given to the National Association of Evangelicals Conference on April 25, 1963. "Forward with Christ in Total Commitment" is a message of the centrality and preeminence of Christ. As listeners, we are challenged to be intelligently, volitionally, exclusively, and irrevocably attached to Christ.

Each can be accessed as a streaming download or Mp3.

ISBN-10: 0-8024-5181-0
ISBN-13: 978-0-8024-5181-1

The world has yet to see what God can do with a man fully consecrated to Him. These words, spoken to D.L. Moody by a fellow evangelist, fired his imagination and gave him a vision for living all out to the glory of God. "By God's help, I aim to be that man," Moody said.

Lyle Dorsett's lucid, thoughtful prose reveals the heart of this great evangelist, recounting his life and realistically probing his strengths, weaknesses, virtues, faults, triumphs, struggles, and motivations to find a man after God's own heart.

"I thoroughly enjoyed each chapter and gladly recommend it. Chapter four alone, on Moody and the Civil War, is worth the price of the book."

~George Sweeting,
Chancellor Emeritus, Moody Bible Institute